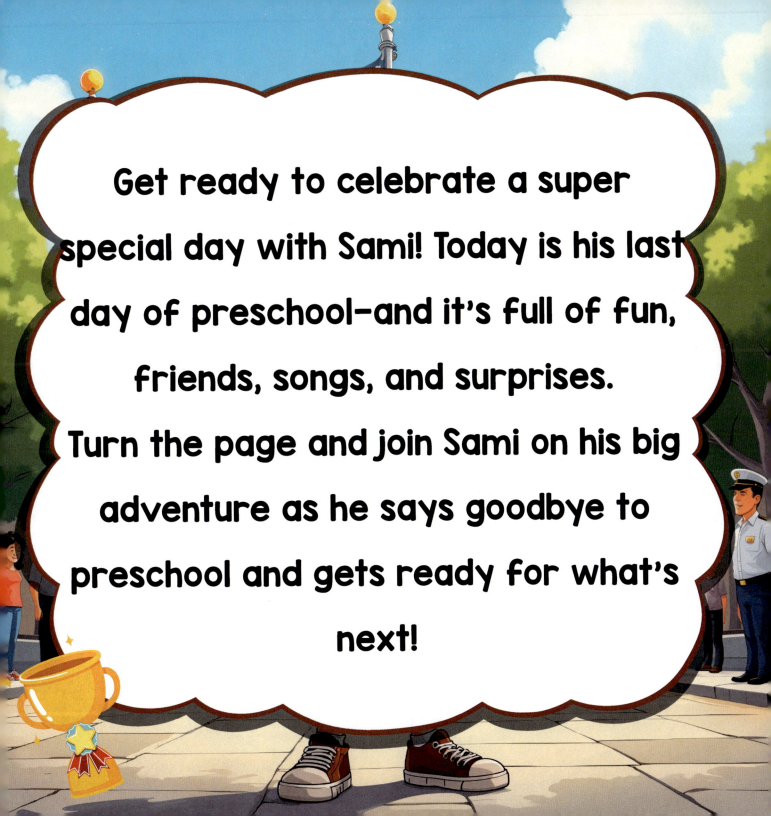

Get ready to celebrate a super special day with Sami! Today is his last day of preschool—and it's full of fun, friends, songs, and surprises. Turn the page and join Sami on his big adventure as he says goodbye to preschool and gets ready for what's next!

THE BIG DAY BEGINS

Sami, a curious boy , jumped out of bed with excitement. He wore his favorite blue T-shirt, brown shorts, and white sneakers. Today was the last day of preschool, and his school had a big graduation ceremony planned!

At breakfast, Sami could barely sit still. He stuffed a pancake into his mouth and wiggled in his chair. "I can't wait to sing on stage!" he cheered. His excitement bubbled over as he grabbed his backpack and dashed out the door. His heart thumped with anticipation—today was going to be special!

Sami raced to school, his sneakers slapping against the sidewalk. The school was decorated with balloons and a giant banner that read 'Congratulations, Preschool Graduates!'. His best friend Mia waved from the classroom door. 'Ready to be big kids?' she asked. Sami grinned. 'Ready as ever!'

THE REHEARSAL MISHAP

Inside the classroom, Sami and his friends lined up for rehearsal. Their teacher, Ms. Green, clapped her hands. 'Alright, everyone, let's practice the song!' Sami took a deep breath and–ACHOO! His sneeze sent his paper graduation cap flying across the room!

Mia giggled as she picked up Sami's cap. 'Maybe you should practice sneezing quieter!' she joked. Sami laughed, putting the cap back on. The class sang their song again, this time without sneezes—until someone's tummy rumbled! The whole room burst into laughter.

Ms. Green shook her head, smiling. 'Let's take a snack break before the real show.' Sami grabbed a juice box and took a big sip. 'This is the best last day ever!' he said. The class agreed, munching happily before their big moment on stage.

THE SOLUTION

HOMEOPROPHYLAXIS:
The Vaccine Alternative

A Parent's Guide to
Educating your Child's
Immune System

2nd edition

Kate Birch, RSHom(NA), CCH

Cilla Whatcott, HD (RHom), CCH

Illustrated by Hannah Albert, ND

ISBN: 9798850190453

Because of the dynamic nature of the Internet, any web addresses or links contained in this book may have changed since publication and may no longer be valid. The views expressed in this work are solely those of the author and do not necessarily reflect the views of the publisher, and the publisher hereby disclaims any responsibility for them.

Any people depicted in stock imagery provided by Thinkstock are models, and such images are being used for illustrative purposes only. Certain stock imagery © Thinkstock.

Hannah Albert created cover and chapter cover images. All other watercolor images on the back cover and in the interior were painted by Kate Birch.

Printed in the United States of America

Dedicated to the health of the human family

Also, by Kate Birch

Vaccine Free Prevention and Treatment of Infectious Contagious Disease with Homeopathy

~

Homoeopathic Treatment of the Liver and Biliary Ducts ~ The Amazing Liver: Interfacing Nature with Spirit

~

The Best Family Homeopathy Acute Care Manual

~

Glyphosate Free: An Essay on Functional Nutrition and the Homeopathic Clearing of Glyphosate Toxicity

~

Long-term Homoeoprophylaxis Study in Children in North America: Part One and Two

Also, by Cilla Whatcott

There is a Choice: Homeoprophylaxis

"The introduction of homeopathy forced the old-school doctor to stir around and learn something of a rational nature about his business. You may honestly feel grateful that homeopathy survived the attempts of the allopaths to destroy it."

Mark Twain, Harper's Bazaar, 1890

Table of Contents

Foreword – Michele Denize Strachan, MD

As a parent and a pediatrician, I invite you to read this book because, to give the best care to our children in an increasingly complex world, we must seek answers from more than one source, and be willing at times to think outside the box.

Twenty-three years ago, when my daughter was born in a water birth at home, I was intent on a non-violent entry into this life for her. Because of my focus on gentleness in the early months of life, I did not want to expose her to either the physical pain or the artificial nature of vaccinations. It was tough for me. Yes, I had the knowledge that gave me the confidence that I could take care of her; on the other hand, I was very isolated and alone since my peers did not understand my concerns or actions. If you are deciding to walk to the beat of your own truth about vaccinations or any other issue in the health of your child, read this book.

It is a fresh voice for parents of young families. The authors take you by the hand, through a different interpretation of familiar concepts such as illness, infection, and fever, to a place where you can trust the promptings of an intuitive nudge toward the decisions that make the most sense to you.

At the University of Minnesota where I work in the Behavioral Pediatrics program, there is an eight-month waiting list. A great many of these children are under 6 years old and challenged by an unexpected twist in the development of attention, motivation, or regulation of emotion, mood, or behavior. Their parents are wondering: "is she/he normal? Will this go away with maturity?" and increasingly, "What can we do without using medications?" Parents are definitely searching for alternatives. If you are one of the searching - whether the subject of your search is development, nutrition, or vaccine alternative – this is a wonderful guide to illuminate your quest, inform your mind, and encourage you along the way.

This book does guide clearly that tricky decision about how, when, and why to choose a viable option to vaccinate your children. In addition, it is studded with gems such as the fact that we share the planet with bacteria and viruses; a truly integrated view of your children's neurological, immune, and social development. As you read this book, allow the authors' blend of wisdom and scientific information to nurture, and inspire you.

Michele Denize Strachan, MD
Behavioral Pediatrician
Developmental Behavioral Pediatrics Clinic
University of Minnesota
April 2012

Foreword – Tetyana Obukhanych, PhD

My disillusionment with vaccination as a method of disease prevention has grown over the years of being a PhD student (at the Rockefeller University, New York, NY) and later a postdoctoral research scientist in immunology at several top U.S. institutions for biomedical research (Immune Disease Institute at Harvard Medical School, Boston, MA and Stanford University School of Medicine, Stanford, CA).

I started out my path in science as an enthusiastic, albeit rather naïve, supporter of vaccination. My pro-vaccine views were based on having no apparent reason to doubt the immunologic theories that are taught in PhD programs and medical schools.

Yet, over time reason for doubt crept in. As I worked in various labs, I had observed outcomes of some experiments that did not fit into conventional immunologic paradigms, yet they were disregarded and not publicized. I had observed extreme emotional insecurity of my colleagues when the subject of discussion would touch upon the negative implications of new research studies on the perceived value of vaccination. As a young scientist, I could not comprehend why the field was so desperately guarding its old dogmas and its outdated invention (vaccines) instead of being open to a sincere and truthful discussion that might lead to a breakthrough in our understanding of immunity.

Over the years, I have come to realize that conventional immunology simply cannot provide real answers as to what constitutes natural immunity to infectious disease, that the theory that supports vaccination is deeply flawed, and that we must seek the answers beyond immunology and beyond vaccines. I am grateful to the pioneers in the field of homeoprophylaxis (HPx) for leading us towards a different paradigm of immunity. I sincerely hope that further research will expand their findings on the effectiveness and safety of HPx in disease prevention, and that it will rightfully replace the vaccination method.

Tetyana Obukhanych, PhD
Author of *Vaccine Illusion*
April 2012

Preface

Every parent wants to ensure the best health for their child. Well baby visits are designed to fulfill this promise; however, these appointments are filled with the doctor's insistence upon vaccination for the health of their child. New families may have not yet considered the many preventative health care options available to them prior to meeting with their doctor.

With the increased capacity of the world-wide web over the last few decades, health information has become more accessible than ever. The frightening prevailing climate in the health care industry includes the exposure of unscrupulous political, monetary, and corporate actions, the realization of harmful environmental influences and the reality of potential risks associated with pharmaceutical drugs. When it comes to your health, it's no longer easy to be satisfied by simple assurances that something is safe, or true.

The government's recommendations for increasing numbers of vaccines for our children has engendered skepticism amongst parents whose interests are solely the long-term health and safety of their children. As parents clamor for accurate information to make wise choices, they are either placated by propaganda from the pharmaceutical companies or scolded by their doctors. Parents are only seeking a solution to the conflicting messages of ever-increasing vaccines against the backdrop of a meteoric rise in pervasive developmental delays, allergies, and behavioral problems in children.

We live in a culture that asks us to take responsibility for not only our families health, but - when it comes to infectious disease - to partake in prevention programs so that, for the benefit of society, we all work towards keeping disease incidence down. Without any other option, it may look like vaccination is the only way to serve this purpose. What we are proposing is another method of disease prevention that is not attended with the risks associated with vaccination, but serves to satisfy these larger public health needs.

Homeoprophylaxis (HPx) is a time-honored practice since the inception of homeopathy in the early eighteen hundreds. Homeopathy is also no stranger to infectious disease. Its effectiveness is well-documented. Many homeopaths have successfully faced epidemics over the last 200 years armed with simple remedies called nosodes, which resolved these epidemics with phenomenal results. Derived from natural sources, nosodes, in combination with other homeopathic remedies, are amazing in their capacity to heal the sick. Our purpose in compiling this book is to share a viable alternative – a solution to the fear and confusion surrounding the vaccine debate.

There is a safe and effective solution to educating our children's immune systems. By sharing our homeopathic thinking as it relates to infectious disease, we aim to present a deeper understanding of the role of infectious disease. By empowering you as a parent with knowledge and education about the immune system, we offer you a safe and gentle method of protection, and a solution to the middle-of-the-night worry that dwells in the heart of every parent with a sick and crying child.

There is a solution!

Kate Birch

Cilla Whatcott

April, 2012

Preface to the Second Edition

By the time we first published this book we determined that we needed a central organization to provide access to Homeoprophylaxis (HPx). As a result, Free and Healthy Children International (FHCi) was created and became a 501(c)3 non-profit to take this work to the next level. The mission of FHCi is research, education, and access to HPx. By establishing and fostering an education platform, a network of support systems overseeing and supervising families undertaking HPx, and the completion of two major research projects in the last ten years, we have taken the little-known practice of HPx into the larger terrain of immunization options, and a household word, for those wanting to keep their immune systems intact in the face of infectious disease.

The findings from these research projects have exponentially expanded our understanding of infectious disease and how HPx works. This second edition has updated and expanded upon many concepts discussed in the first addition; You will find a historical survey of the comparison between germ and terrain theories; there are new sections on the healthy biome, the interrelationship between the health of the mother's and infants' biome, and the implications of man-made viruses and mRNA vaccines; Discussed more extensively is the relationship of the immune system to the environment and how the natural suppression of the mother's and fetal immune systems in gestation are a part of that relationship.

The chapter on homeoprophylaxis has been expanded an updated to include the immunological benefits of each disease in the Full Childhood Immunological HPx Program; Included also are descriptions of 7 new HPx programs; Questions and Answers have been updated to reflect the new HPx Programs, an increased understanding of HPx, and some of the effects of the recent global pandemic; Additionally, international research results have been added including the FHCi long-term research papers on childhood HPx and coronavirus prevention; Discussions on public health policy have been revised to address some of the failings exposed from creation and mis-management of the Covid-19 global pandemic; Finally, the index has been updated and additional references have been added to validify research.

All of this is to say that this second edition is a testament to how we are paying attention. The concepts conveyed are the result of 80-100 practitioners working in constant dialog over the years of supervising HPx as well as navigated the clinical management of Covid-19 and vaccine fallout. While the original explanation of immune function and the effects of Homeoprophylaxis system ring true from the first edition, development of new HPx programs give us a new frontier to set our eyes upon. If you are new to Homeoprophylaxis, welcome. If you are a seasoned practitioner, may you find gems of inspiration for your practice. If you have been with us all along thank you.

In service. Kate Birch, July 1, 2023

Acknowledgments

Our deepest thanks and acknowledgement go to Dr. Isaac Golden for his pioneering fifteen-year study of homeoprophylaxis (HPx). With his permission, we have included some of his results. We also extend our sincere thanks to all those who have gone before in their work of bringing homeopathy to light for the benefit of mankind. We especially thank those homeopaths around the continent who currently support us in our endeavor to make the content of this book a reality. Thank you to Kristin Linner, PhD, for her help and guidance in helping to clarify various aspects of the immune system from her dual expertise as a homeopath and former immunologist. Thanks to Michele Strachan, MD, for her guidance and input as a pediatrician, mother, and advocate of holistic health, for her insights and concerns regarding organization, layout, and content. Thank you to Abby Magnus for her help in the final proof. Thanks to Tetyana Obukhanych, PhD, for the support of our work and graciousness in contributing a foreword.

Thank you, Ursula Dobelmann, for your contributions and final proof of the second edition. Your mirror and confirmation of the concepts and experience in homeoprophylaxis have been invaluable to the second edition.

We thank the growing community of homeopaths who are bringing knowledge and understanding of Homeoprophylaxis (HPx) to their practices and making it accessible to inquiring families and communities around the world. We thank the parents who have entrusted the system of homeopathy with the health and welfare of their children. It is you who are forging a path towards the future. Your children will be strong, healthy contributing members of society as a result. May all who partake in HPx benefit.

Thank you to our own families and children for their patience with us as we continue to pursue this life-long quest to serve humanity.

Introduction

The decision not to vaccinate for many parents is a difficult one. It often starts with mothers having an intuitive feeling that vaccination is just not right. Their babies are so small and fragile, how can it be good to load their systems with multiple injected doses of pathogenic material? Pressure from husbands, doctors, parents, and in-laws can make these women feel unsubstantiated in their gut feelings. Sometimes the decision to vaccinate is postponed. Yet there remains the fear that their children will not be able to go to school without state required shots. What if their child gets sick? What is one to do?

At the root of these questions is how are we to keep our children healthy and how can we support the development of their immune systems if we are to stimulate immunity and prevent disease?

Our inspiration stems from our desire to provide new families and their relatives with a quick and easy guide to understanding their children's immune system, its development and response to sickness, and how best to prevent infectious disease. While allopathic medicine is unable to offer any alternatives to antibiotics and vaccines in the treatment or prevention of these potentially dangerous diseases, homeopathy and homeoprophylaxis (HPx) offer a safe, inexpensive, and effective alternative.

Throughout the book, we will introduce homeopathic understanding of the disease process. Rather than being a manual for homeopathic treatment, this book serves as a transition guide from the conventional view of infectious disease to a more holistic way of thinking, highlighting the role of infectious diseases as immune system educators.

While the common view of acute disease is that it should be avoided at all costs, (the current use of vaccination is to these ends) we have forgotten the possible positive role acute disease can play. To fully educate your children's immune system, we believe we need to capture the benefits of disease without succumbing to the suffering of the disease. HPx provides a proactive measure while capturing these benefits.

Accordingly, the contents herein are not about how to use HPx to stop acute disease. But rather how the systematic use of homeopathic nosodes replaces the need for active acute disease and actually stimulates a greater level of health. We call this immune system education. We say, 'let life work with HPx.'

Herein we invite you to explore a holistic view of disease, your child's developing immune system and how we can best serve it. We will be examining some strongly held cultural beliefs about sickness, whether bacteria or viruses are the cause of disease or result, the concept of herd immunity, and thoughtfully question whether the production of antibodies should be the only goal in a disease prevention method.

As you may be introduced to some new concepts, it may take some time to assimilate them.

If the goal is to give a tiny and harmless dose of the disease to initiate immunity, how can we stay true to this vision with a disease prevention method without harming our children?

Outline

- What is infectious disease, overview of the immune system, its development, and the beneficial role of fevers and the relationship between the mothers' and infants' biomes and immune systems.
- Introduction and overview of HPx as an alternative to vaccination for preventing infectious contagious disease.
- Questions and Answers on HPx.
- Discussions will show how HPx effectively stimulates the immune system towards immunity without the subsequent side-effects vaccines cause and captures the benefits of acute disease without the attended suffering.
- Discussions on new HPx programs for improved health in all ages.
- Discussions on the method and problems of vaccination.
- Overview of clinical findings of HPx around the world and mechanisms of access to HPx.
- Comparing and contrasting the current methodology of vaccination with homeoprophylaxis (HPx).
- A reference of acute diseases and related remedies to the commonly-vaccinated-against-diseases, sexually transmitted disease, and tropical diseases (for those that wish to travel overseas).

Because you have taken the time to research this subject matter and to question information in the public domain, we believe that you will find the answers you are looking for herein.

What is Infectious Contagious Disease?

Pathogens and humans have evolved together over eons

The Interaction of Bacteria and Viruses with Humans

Bacteria and viruses have evolved over time in relationships with humans. Man, as a complex DNA replication system, not separate from the earth, nature's laws or the single celled bacteria that are housed in his body is a result of the complex evolutionary relationship between himself and these intelligent beings.

Humans, whose consciousness, thought forms, metabolic processes, immune system regulation processes, hormonal and neurotransmitter production are a direct function of their relationship to the commensal bacteria that populate their intestinal lining. When the self is aligned in relationship to nature and these bacteria, the vital force and expression of the immune system is the direct manifestation of the vital force of the bacteria housed. Man, capable of rendering the finest music, scholarly achievements, and global exploration, is the same Man stricken by poverty, perversion, and war. Bacterial populations vary in different cultures based upon the food he eats, the wine he drinks, and the medicine he chooses.

Bacteria and viruses have come and gone in epidemics and scourges based on varying collective susceptibilities in those human populations. These same bacteria and viruses have shaped cultures, religious behaviors, and rituals throughout history.

The contagious infectious disease process activates an immune system response between the human body and the immunological agent that can be passed from one person to another. Modern science believes bacteria and viruses are the cause of these infectious contagious diseases. Terrain theory postulates it is the susceptibility of the person that dictates contraction, the no-virus theory suggests that the immunological processes produced are detoxification processes of the body.

Our understanding is that infectious agents are intelligent beings that serve to activate an evolutionary process in the individual and collective through the exonerative process of a fever and discharge.

In some instances, however the intensity of that immunological process is so violent as to kill the person or leave them damaged for life.

Epidemics of disease have acted as checks and balances in the human population, throughout time, based upon human frailties within the environment they exist and errors of living. The action of pathogens can be seen as pressure release valves for situations and environments not conducive to sustaining human life, either for the individual, or the larger population. Those with poor nutrition, living in over-crowded or unsanitary conditions, or those under certain political and social pressures have a much greater susceptibility to contracting disease specific to that susceptibility. The weaker, the old, and the young, and those living outside of the natural laws of this existence are at greater risk of complications in these disease processes.

While it is not the pathogen itself that directly causes the complication, it is the reaction, or lack of reaction of the human body to the pathogen that dictates the course the disease will follow. How high the fever goes,

how violent the purgative process is, etc., governs how an individual will fare through an illness.

Those who contract the disease, display a moderate symptom picture, and survive the process are often gifted with life-long immunity, greater freedom from chronic disease, and greater developmental maturity from having undergone the process.

Historically, until the development of homeopathy, there has never been any reliable system of medicine that facilitates this process of immune response. Rather, avoidance of infectious disease was necessary to limit disease outbreaks. Advancements in sanitary practices, clean water and food, better nutritional status and living conditions have all made the greatest impact in reducing disease incidence.[1]

None-the-less, the human immune system is well equipped to recognize and develop appropriate immune system responses to naturally occurring pathogens because our co-evolutionary journey has encrypted in our DNA the immunological mechanisms of this process.

Holism

The holistic view of disease observes that when the environment of the individual is mal-tuned, then, and only then, will the person become sick from the external environment.

This mal-tuned internal environment then opens the door for a disease agent to invite an immunological response to re-tune the individual.

Thus, the role of the disease agent is to re-tune the internal environment through the immune process that is activated.

While the conventional approach is to destroy all potential pathogens and shore up the immune system with vaccinations to avoid any pathological process, the holistic approach is to strengthen the individual, to make him less susceptible to getting sick. Then if sickness does occur, to help the immune system make the sufficient and required action to rectify the situation.

The use of antibiotics or genetically modified viral vaccines, have given us a false belief that we can, or have, eradicated certain disease processes. While vaccination may eliminate the pathogenetic expression of a particular disease, and antibiotics may kill some pathogens, we must remember these entities have intelligence and their own imperative to survive. Additionally, they will mutate to ensure their survival. Moreover, the paradigm of vaccination misses the point that infectious disease offers humans the opportunity of evolution if their message is delivered in the appropriate dose. Homeopathic potentization renders

the message to a from it can be realized by the living organism.

As humans have changed the evolutionary course of viruses through genetic manipulation, viral strains have mutated, and through excessive use of antibiotics, bacteria have become 'super bugs'[2] infectious disease continues.

Neither the use of antibiotics or vaccines has improved the immunological process of the individual; we have not solved the problem of susceptibility, nor do they give credence to the need for the disease process.

It is the balance between immune system response and virulence of the pathogen that dictates the course of the infective process.

Germ Theory, Terrain Theory, Frequency Amplification, No-Virus Theory, and Susceptibility

Some historical perspective is needed to understand the difference between germ, terrain, and the no-virus theories.

- **Germ theory** postulates that all disease manifestation is a result of a germ (bacteria or virus)
- **Terrain theory** postulates that it is the environment (susceptibility) of the individual that sets the stage for infectious disease to manifest.
- **The no-virus (exosome) theory** of infectious disease claims it is the human response to a toxic external environment that activates a discharge process and liberation of outdated genetic material that looks like an infectious disease process and viral shedding.

The following individuals have played key roles in studying the nature of potentially pathogenic organisms, their interactions in human populations, and the development of methodologies for prevention and treatment. Identification bacteria and viruses was not developed till the late1800's, regardless of identification the implications of these pathogens have led to divergent understandings of disease manifestation, contagion justification, and treatment and prevention modalities.

Edward Jenner: May 17, 1749 – January 26, 1823: England. One of the first to study infectious diseases. He studied smallpox and developed a cow pox vaccine (root word – Vacca, for cow). It was observed that those who had contracted cowpox were immune to smallpox. He postulated that by giving everyone cowpox we could eradicate smallpox.

Samuel Hahnemann: April 10, 1755 – July 2, 1843: Germany and France. A vitalist and the developer of the system of homeopathy, postulated that contagion was a result of a magnetic field of a sick person that influenced individuals near to them that affected contagion.

Hahnemann developed the Genus Epidemicus (GE) model of disease prevention: stating any remedy that could be matched to the symptom presentation of an infectious disease, that also was shown to be effective in the treatment that disease, could prevent the same disease. GE is a form of Homeoprophylaxis and can be accomplished with either a nosode or a remedy if the totality of symptoms of the epidemic correspond to the totality of symptoms of the medicament.

Samuel Hahnemann – Memorial, Washington DC.

Antoine Béchamp: October 16, 1816 – April 15, 1908: France. Who defined terrain theory, understood that it was the soil (terrain) of the individual that determined if the individual got sick or not upon exposure to other affected people.

Louis Pasteur: December 27, 1822 – September 28,1895: France. Was credited for the development of germ theory and the first discovery of microbes under a microscope. This theory is the main accepted scientific theory for infectious diseases. It states that microorganisms, pathogens or "germs" are the cause of disease: these small organisms, too small to be seen without magnification, invade humans, other animals, and other living hosts. Their growth and reproduction within their hosts can cause disease.

"Germ" refers to not just a bacterium but to any type of microorganism, such as protists or fungi, or even non-living pathogens that can cause disease, such as viruses, prions, or viroids.

While studying rabies and attempting to make a rabies vaccine in the mid 1800's, he was perplexed by the conundrum that after being injected with the blood from an actively rabid dog's blood the subject dogs all died. This idea of using the disease that was incubated in another living species to weaken or 'attenuate' the disease seemed brilliant and so he began his trials with rabies virus incubated in live rabbits. Sure enough, the serum procured from the,

now dead rabbits, was weakened enough so that it was able to produce an immunological response in dogs but not strong enough to kill them. And thus, out of this study, the practice of attenuating viruses on animal host mediums the production of vaccines began. Interestingly the Rabies nosode was the first nosode made by Hahnemann himself.

At the end of his life, **Louis Pasteur** revoked his stake on the germ theory and postulates, in his private diaries he states unequivocally that in his entire career he was not once able to transfer disease from one to another with a pure culture of bacteria and concurred that is was in fact the terrain of the individual that determined if an individual got sick or not.

James Compton Burnett: July 10, 1840 – April 2, 1901: England. Was a homeopath who studied the adverse effects of smallpox vaccines (made from cowpox), he cataloged and defined the first instances of vaccinosis from these vaccines, and championed homeoprophylaxis. He determined that the use of diluted disease agents was a more rational system of disease prevention. He further stated that it was the similitude of cowpox effect on the human system that actually was the reason for its ability to prevent smallpox because it was actually curing the susceptibility to that disease in the individual: According to the Law of Similars, that which can produce a set of symptoms can also cure that same set of symptoms.

Robert Koch: December 1, 1843 – May 27, 1910: England. He developed Koch's Postulates: four criteria designed to establish a causal relationship between a microbe and a disease.

Koch's four postulates are:

- The microorganism must be found in abundance in all organisms suffering from the disease but should not be found in healthy organisms.
- The microorganism must be isolated from a diseased organism and grown in pure culture.
- Cultured microorganisms should cause disease when introduced into a healthy organism.
- The microorganism must be re-isolated from the inoculated, diseased experimental host and identified as being identical to the original specific causative agent.

Dr. Luc Montagnier: August 18, 1932 – February 8, 2022: France. He was the discoverer of HIV and determined that solutions of infectious agents emitted certain frequencies and if a solution with an infectious agent was diluted it still emitted that frequency, and further that if a blank vessel was subjected to that frequency the same infectious agent would manifest in this vessel. He was able to prove the energetic quality of infectious agents. He went on further to study the effects of the Polymerase Chain Reaction (PCR) processes applied to these solutions to enhance viral replication.[3]

Thomas Cowan: October 1956 – current: USA. Was a 30-year medical doctor who lost his medical license due to practicing outside of conventional medical institutions' practice guidelines, postulated the no-virus theory of infection. He studied the synchronicity between the activation of 5G cellular frequencies in Wuhan, China, in December of 2019 with the outbreak of Covid-19. Iran and Italy had the next highest incidence of disease expression and similarly activated 5G in early 2020. He also claimed that, as no viral particle has ever been identified for Covid-19, but that sputum samples contained exosomes (host generated extra cellular vesical with genetic material looking like viral strands), from sick individuals were the result of the adaptation process to 5G exposure and liberation of the hosts genetic material.[4]

Kate Birch RSHom(NA), CCH: March 8, 1964 – current: USA. She is a homeopath and infectious disease specialist who, through research and clinical applications of HPx understands that susceptibility to infectious disease is an aspect of the constitution of the individual and that active infectious disease processes are meant to satisfy some susceptibilities. She also postulated that groups of people succumb to infectious disease because groups can suffer from a similar cumulative vibrational state that is relative to the environment, political systems they live within, thought forms, beliefs, genetic inheritances, and lifestyle choices. This vibrational state if not in alignment with nature acts as a vacuum for an infectious agent to manifest. The immune system response generated is intended to activate and transmute the limitations of that non-functional state for the benefit of the health of the individual and if collectively processed, for the benefit of humanity.[5]

Thus, Genesis 2:7: *"Then the lord GOD formed the man of the dust of the ground and breathed into his nostrils the breath of life; and the man became a living soul."*

The dust of life includes all elements, plants, animals, microbes bacteria, fungi, mold, and viruses.

Disease Prevention Models

Different prevention and treatment medical models have been established based on all these theories. This book discusses all, but most importantly, exposés the benefits of the energetic system of homeopathy for treatment of, and homeoprophylaxis for prevention of infectious disease: both operate at the level of susceptibility of the individual.

Summary

- **Antibiotics** are used to kill bacteria but do nothing to change the environment of the host.
- **Modern vaccines** are used to force an immunological response to a virus or bacteria towards antibody production at the expense of altered immune response
- **Homeopathy** uses energetic renditions of substances that can produce the same symptoms as an infectious disease to treat the disease: Law of Similars.
- **The homeoprophylaxis (HPx) method**, which can be used for both bacterial and viral presentation, shares the same theory as vaccines but uses an energetic form of the disease agent to facilitate rebalancing the terrain. The result captures the evolutionary benefit of that process.
- **Detoxification programs** have been set up to increase the vitality of the person to reduce the need for an infectious agent to activate the same purification process.

Healthy Biomes Engender Healthy Lives

The vital force, consciousness, thought forms, metabolism, and immunological functions of the human mammal are a direct result of the functioning and vitality of the commensal bacteria and their interface with the intestinal lining. The biome includes bacteria that cover the surface of our bodies and all mucous membranes. Our vitality is reflective of the natural vitality of the biome within us.

As humans are lactating mammals, lacto-fermenting bacteria are essential for most all biological processes. The most dominant bacterial phyla in the human biome belong to the genera Bacteroides, Clostridia, Faecalibacterium, Eubacterium, Peptococcus, Peptostreptococcus, Streptococcus, Staphylococcus, and Bifidobacteria. Other genera, such as Eschericha (E. coli) and Lactobacillus are present to a lesser extent. Species from the genus Bacteroides alone constitute about 30% of all bacteria in the gut, suggesting that this genus is especially important.

The biome is responsible for facilitating multiple functions including, but not limited to, metabolism and digestive processes, hormonal regulation, immune system function, neurotransmitter production and regulation, blood clotting, behavior and learning, and normal childhood development. Bacteria on the skin enable it to heal and prevents opportunistic infections from invasive species. Probiotics are a necessary and healthy contribution to every diet to keep bacterial populations in check.

Bacteria

Bacteria are unicellular organisms of all shapes and sizes. They are present in every environment. Bacteria are vital in recycling nutrients from the atmosphere and through decomposition. The commensal bacteria present in human digestive tracts are responsible for the functionality of multiple systems within the body. Bacteria are used for many food preserving techniques, such as the making of cheeses and yogurt.

As the DNA of bacteria is not encapsulated in a nuclear membrane, bacteria can transfer bits of DNA, a replicon, from one to the other to facilitate survival. Accordingly, bacteria can 'learn' from each other how to survive in oil spills, radioactive soil, and antibiotic mediums.

Healthy bacteria can become pathological when the environment of the human changes or when they inhabit the wrong organ system, i.e., surgical wounds, bacterial meningitis. Other bacteria such as cholera and tuberculosis are always pathological and hygiene methods should be employed to avoid contact. However, in outbreaks of disease, we must endeavor to understand why certain individuals are susceptible to pathogens while others are not.

High fevers and discharges are needed to kill overpopulating bacteria. Reduction of a fever during a bacterial infection can lead to further invasion.

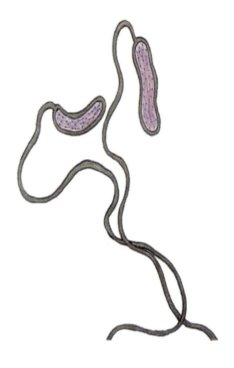

Bacterium Vibrio cholerae

Antibiotics

There are three main classes of antibiotics

- Sulpha containing compounds. These antibiotics work to interrupt an enzymatic metabolic process of bacteria, thus starving them. Sulphonamides can cause severe allergic reactions.
- Semi-synthetic drugs made in the laboratory from a synthesis of naturally occurring substances, in combination with a beta-lactam molecule. Penicillin contains a beta-lactam molecule. Side-effects include hives, diarrhea, or systemic Candida.
- Streptomyces are a type of naturally occurring bacteria that, when given orally inhibit the growth of pathogenic bacterial, fungal, and other parasitic infections. Streptomycin, Nystatin, and Neomycin are examples. Side-effects include damage to the inner ear, allergic reactions, or kidney damage, respectively.
- Antibiotics drive Candida over-growth.

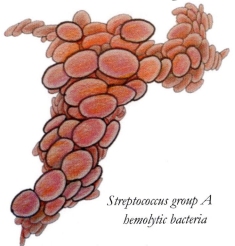

Streptococcus group A hemolytic bacteria

Candida Albicans

When healthy bacteria are displaced, pathological bacteria and Candida multiply. Candida is a yeast. Populations of it are normal within the human system, however repetitive use of antibiotics promotes over-growth. High Candida environments produce alcohol through their formation process. It makes the body more acidic leading to inflammation, brain fog, bloating, fermented stools, and causes intense sugar and alcohol cravings, and the tendency to gain weight.

Antibiotics are used to kill *Streptococcal* bacteria. In their place, Clostridium difficile or Candida overgrowth occurs. Over time as the normal bacterial balance attempts to reestablish itself (including healthy Streptococcal bacteria) a fever develops. This fever is asking the individual to get their internal environment so as to live in harmony with Bifido and lacto-fermenting bacteria populations (*Streptococcal bacteria* are lacto-fermenting). With continued use of antibiotics the *Streptococcal bacteria* become antibiotic-resistant, thus becoming more virulent. In addition, heightened auto-immune responses develop such as rheumatic fever, nephritis, or PANS or PANDAS.

When the individual and their biome is in balance, health is maintained, systems are properly regulated, cognitive processes are in sync with reality, and vitality is felt.

Fungi, Yeasts, and Molds

Fungi, yeasts, and molds are found mostly on dead or decomposing matter. They have been used as food, such as mushrooms, and in a variety of food production methods, such as cheese and beer making. They also can cause food spoilage. Most fungi are non-pathogenic, but individuals with severely compromised immune systems can become host to a variety of molds or fungi.

Penicillium are a type of fungi that cause the spoilage of seeds and other stored foods. Abundant growth of *penicillium* hinders the growth of other bacteria. This observation brought the use of penicillin into medicine for the control of bacterial infections.

While occasional use of the penicillin, or other antibiotics, may kill bacteria that have become pathogenic, there will always be some that survive. Repeated use of penicillin leads to drug resistant strains of bacteria and over-growth of yeast in the individual. Yeast over-growth, interferes with metabolic function, digestion, and cognitive function.

Penicillium notatum

Mothers' Biome Dictates the Biome of the Infant

Biome health is passed from mother to child in utero. Bacteroides and lactobacillus populations are a part of normal, healthy mother's placental and vaginal microbiome.

The mother's biome is a result of her mothers' biome, and her grandmother's biome. Memory of episodes of starvation, gastrointestinal disease, international and cultural metabolic influences in the genetic line, or the number of antibiotics will be held in the commensal populations and will influence the biome of the infant.

Both the placenta and amniotic fluid contain the mothers' commensal bacteria. Suckling at the breast, with contact to the mother's skin and ingesting first colostrum and subsequent mother's milk, sets the foundation of the fetus's digestive tract.

Excessive use of antibiotics in the mother will drive out lacto-fermenting bacteria, increase Candida and lead to biome dysregulation in the child which can lead to developmental delays and immune system dysregulation.

Viruses

Viruses consist of a single or double strand of DNA or RNA and a viral coat. Some say that viruses are the cause of disease, others say they are result of disease. The human immune system will respond to either the viral genetic material or to markers in the protein coat. Once a virus is activated, the viral RNA or DNA strands overtake the cell for replication. Retroviruses can enter the host's DNA, where they will lay dormant until the host becomes sufficiently stressed, resulting in an outbreak, and resurfacing of disease symptoms.

Moderate fevers are required to stimulate antibodies which will bind with the viral components. Immune system cells will localize these foreign particles, and work to engulf and remove them from the body via discharges, eruptions, or through the large intestine in the stool.

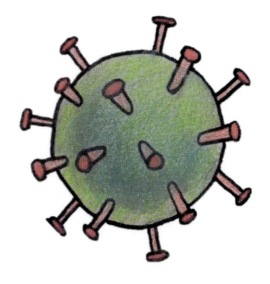

Influenza virus

Man-Made Viruses

Since the publication of the first edition of this book the world has been struck by Covid-19. In the three years since the first cases, we have seen the virus devolve to becoming less and less virulent. This is the nature of RNA viruses. Each time an immunological process is activated by an individual due to the nature of RNA viruses and their ability to transform and be transformed by the hosts cellular replication, the genetics of that RNA strand changes.

The understanding is that the spike protein is a compilation of multiple viral and bacterial strains of genetic information touching upon and activating previous susceptibility of the infected. Accordingly, immune responses to man-made viruses are difficult for the body to overcome.

Creation of Vaccines

Vaccines are created by either separating the viral coats from the genetic material, through denaturing the genetic material to hinder viral replication, or through genetically modified viruses and recombinant technology where bits of viral strands are joined with other viral species' strands to weaken or strengthen the virulence of the pathogen.

As viruses for vaccine manufacturing are incubated in animal host cell cultures, research is now showing that bits of the host cell DNA are recombining with the vaccine material.[6] Viral DNA/RNA in the host cell culture is also combining with the vaccine material. These viral particles and animal DNA/RNA are then injected via the vaccines into humans, creating a whole new kind of pathogenic material and subsequent disease process.

What we don't know is whether the immune system is sophisticated enough to make antibodies to laboratory created pathogens, and if not, what kind of disease processes are we likely to encounter as disease agents become more complex and co-mingle with our own genetic blueprint?

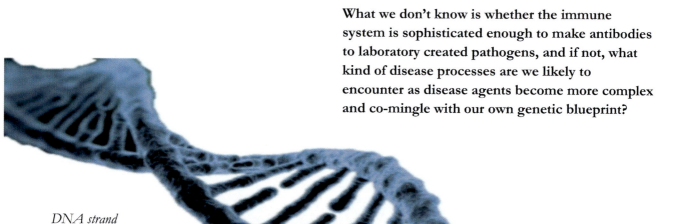

DNA strand

Health is Measured by

- One's ability to adapt to the external pressures of life and the environment
- One's ability to bring physical action into the external environment to create a living situation that is conducive to life and health: socially, spiritually, culturally, politically, and economically.

Disease is Influenced by

Frequency of outbreaks of acute disease is in direct relationship to how a particular environment is limited in certain aspects of human life.

Overexposure to heat, cold, lack of sleep, lack of nourishment or shelter, overcrowding and poverty, political oppression, war etc., all increase susceptibility toward infectious contagious disease processes.

Rather than seeing pathogens as responsible for the disease process, one can say the pathogen survives because of conditions which are conducive to that disease process.

A disease becomes contagious either by its virulence or its existence in a population that shares the same physical, social, religious, cultural, political, or economic susceptibilities.

If the person or group of people develops immunity and survives through the illness, we can say that a level of susceptibility in this individual or group was satisfied by the illness. And if before and after parameters are studied you would also see a transformation of society that reflects the immunological discharge process.

In the largest sense, as we know some people are stronger and possess greater biological conviction after an acute process - we can say that the infectious process functioned as a tonifier and liberator of something deeper in the individual's health.

Role of Acute Disease

The normal process of developing a fever and a discharge liberates the body of toxins. Non-beneficial thought patterns and internal conflicts can build up over time and limit the life-force of a person or group of people. The liberation of those toxins transforms the relationship of the individual(s) to their external environment. This natural exonerative process results in specific immunity which, for some diseases is life-long.

The pathogens implicated in this process could be considered symbiotic towards maintaining the health of the individual if the body's reaction to the pathogen is not so violent as to kill itself in the process.

The symptom expression of a fever and discharge are necessary to eliminate the pathogen. The most effective form of medicine will facilitate the function by increasing the fever and discharge to be fully effective.

In contrast to the allopathic approach of fighting against the body's natural defense mechanism by suppressing fevers, the homeopathic method works towards understanding the meaning and purpose of the symptoms and facilitating this self-correcting mechanism so that the pathogen is eliminated, and harmony is restored to the body.[7]

Not all people, at all times, will succumb to an acute infectious process. Susceptibility is based on two factors: the inherent health of the individual and the virulence of the pathogen. If the susceptibility to acute disease is left unaddressed or suppressed by inappropriate treatment, it will always find a different way to express itself.

Those with weak vitality will produce insufficient fever or eliminatory processes leaving them susceptible to deeper pathological conditions. Those with a strong vitality can produce overly intense symptoms in attempts to rectify the situation causing excess suffering, also putting the person at risk.

Points to Remember

- Bacteria and viruses are evolving life forms.
- We need healthy bacteria to live a healthy life.
- The presence of pathological bacteria is due to a preexisting state of the individual.
- It is the reactive mechanism of the person rather than the actual pathogen that has the potential to cause harm.
- Antibiotics don't create health.
- Vaccines incubated in animal tissue introduce foreign species' DNA into our bodies.
- Healthy immune response is an important part of good health.
- Discharges are detoxification processes.
- The severity of an infectious disease process is equal and opposite to the susceptibility of the individual to that disease.
- Those with a higher susceptibility will either experience greater severity of immunological expression, or insufficient activity, leaving the individual open to damages from the too strong immune response, or incomplete resolution of the disease process from lack of sufficient response.

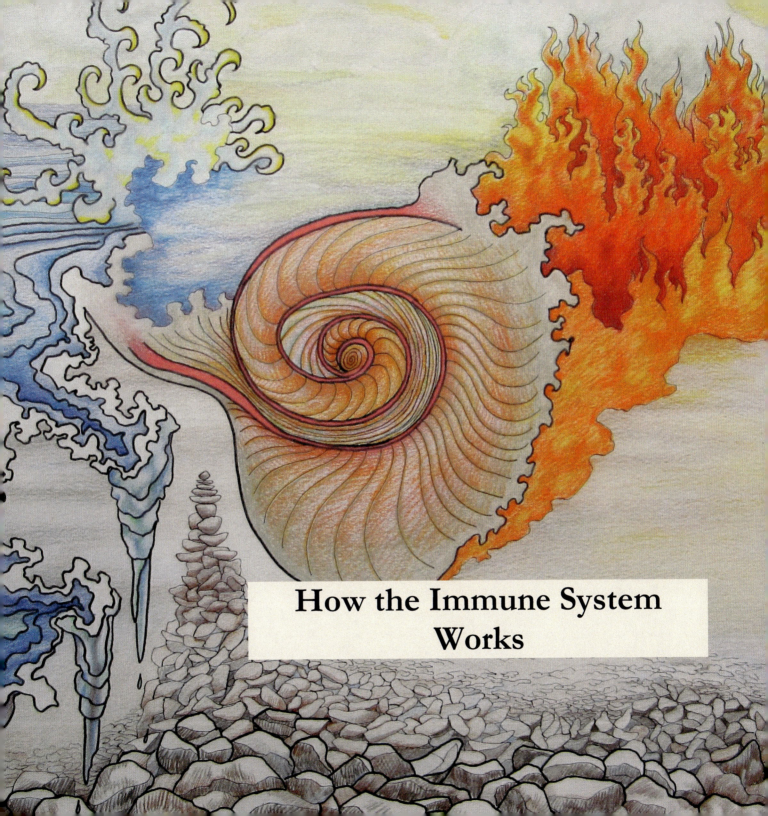

How the Immune System Works

There is perfect order
in the universe
and in the developing
immune system

Development of the Immune System

The immune system is designed to direct us toward the ultimate goal in life – survival and growth while living in an external environment. It is also intent on detoxifying the body through elimination channels of that which does not serve its health. It does so through its natural intelligence, which is a powerful vital force permeating every cell in the body. Immune system development is based on the immune health of the mother and is interconnected with the development of the nervous and digestive systems, alongside the development of the intellect, personality, and social function of the individual.

After nine months of symbiotic life in the womb, Baby emerges as a separate being with his innate immune system intact (general immune system). This system acts as the first line of defense to the outside world in a non-specific manner. The newborn's main challenge is **differentiating self** from **non-self** in relationship to this world. Through exposure to the environment, the immune system determines what is good for the body and what is not, what should be assimilated and what should be eliminated.

From the mother's breast the child receives nourishment along with her antibodies. This passive acquired immunity serves as protection from specific diseases that the mother has antibodies for.

Over time, with exposure to the environment, the child begins to develop his or her own antibodies and memory develops of how to respond to particular antigens.

In the first year, an infant's immune system knows how to localize inflammation, develop a fever, and produce a discharge to eliminate any foreign invader. Runny noses, coughs and eruptions are all evidence of this general immune system activity. Specific antibody production begins by around one year of age and continues to develop over the following years.

This process of maturation continues over the next five to ten years. By the age of six, general and specific immunity is matured in its ability to identify intruders, mount an appropriate febrile defense, develop specific antibodies, and contain, immobilize, and eliminate pathogens from the system.

The natural excretory routes for these discharges are through nasal discharge, expectoration from the lungs, via the stool, or through the skin via perspiration or eruptions.

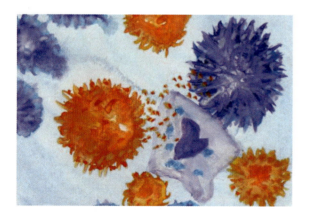

The cycle of inflammation: T cells (orange) communicate via cytokines with other inflammatory cells, such as B cells and macrophages, to maintain, amplify or suppress this cycle.

Overview of the Immune System Cells

The adaptive immune system has two arms – Th1 and Th2 activity, that of cell-mediated or humoral function respectively. This is the critical balance between general and specific immunity.

It is essential for healthy immune system development for these two arms of the immune system to work in coordination with each other to completely resolve each disease process.

Cell-mediated and humoral immune system cells in summary

- Cell-mediated immunity (general immunity)
  T-lymphocytes, Macrophages
  CD8 cytotoxic cells
  CD4 T-helper cells: Th1, neutrophils
- Humoral immunity (antibody specific immunity)
  CD4 T helper cells: Th2
  B-lymphocytes, mast cells, eosinophils, antibody production

Th1 and Th2 helper cells are distinguished by the sets of cytokines they make and the effects that these have on the immune response. Cytokines induce fevers which in turn serve to kill the pathogen. Th1 cells work principally with macrophages in developing a cell-mediated response. Th2 cells stimulate B-cells in developing an antibody-mediated immune response.

Healthy Immune Response

If we think of the process of illness and immune system response in a circular way, we enter the circle upon peripheral **exposure** to a germ. Entry into the body is based upon susceptibility (this is the terrain). A pathogen may have entered through a break in the skin or contact with respiratory tissue or the gastrointestinal tract.

White blood cells in these peripheral linings alert deeper aspects of the immune system to possible intruders (Th1 activity). After exposure, during the incubation of a disease, the **prodrome**, all aspects of the immune system are engaged and activated in identifying the nature of the invasion. The recognition of invaders first takes place on the mucous membranes of the gastrointestinal tract and airways. While no actual symptoms of disease are yet apparent, there may be fussiness, emotional outbursts, and changes in appetite or difficulty sleeping at this stage. During this phase, a **chill** can develop. The chill signals the body to increase its temperature and release calcium from the bones to protect the brain during the fever.

Next a **fever** erupts. This can build slowly over a period of days or suddenly with a high temperature. During the febrile process **antibody** production is initiated to neutralize the pathogen or virus (Th2 activity). Viral illnesses stimulate moderate fevers while bacterial invasions require a high fever to destroy the pathogen.

Additionally, during the fever, white blood cell activity localizes and de-activates the pathogen. A **discharge** or **eruption** follows to remove the antibody/antigen complex out of the body, i.e., the pustules of chickenpox, a loose cough, or purulent runny nose. Next a period of **perspiration** happens as the fever breaks. After which the body finds **resolution** and **cell-mediated immunity**, completing the circle and returning to health. Depending on the disease, this cycle normally takes place over three to twenty-one days from exposure to resolution.

As this cycle repeats itself with different exposures to the natural world, with adaptation immunity is gradually developed, and vitality is enhanced. Major milestones in mental and emotional development occur as resolution takes place.

Fevers must be supported to move it to completion. An intermittent or insufficient fever that never breaks into a sweat is inadequate to move the situation toward resolution.

Antipyretics, like Tylenol or Advil, suppress fevers, never allowing the body to move through all stages towards effective immune system resolution.

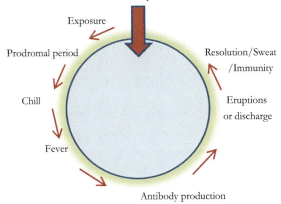

The cycle of healthy immune response

Immune System as Interface to the Environment

The primary purpose of the immune system is to recognize the difference between self and non-self in relation to the external environment. The terrain is the underlaying health and responsiveness of the human system. In health the terrain repels disease energy. The immune system serves as the bridge between the terrain and the germ for sustained immunity. This relationship starts in utero.

Immune System Function During Gestation

The immune systems of both the mother and child are naturally suppressed from the moment the embryo implants into the uterine wall (day 8/9 after fertilization). This natural suppression is to ensure survival of the fetus. The placenta releases Human Chorionic Gonadotropin (HCG) which signals the DNA of the mother to suppress the Th2 response (antibody function) of her immune system making her system naturally Th1 dominant through pregnancy.

For the mother, her immune system is suppressed to not reject the fetus. When the placenta ceases to release HCG towards the end of pregnancy, the dropping levels activate the mothers' immune system to release histamine and serotonin which in turn initiates the hormone stimulation of childbirth. This same mechanism is responsible for early term miscarriages; the placenta fails to produce enough HCG to maintain the pregnancy.

Concurrently, the DNA of the developing embryo regulates the development of its own immune system toward Th1 dominance as well. After the first few sets of cell division fetal DNA begins to code towards cellular differentiation for the formation of the three primary cell layers of the blastocyst. This regulatory control system maintains suppression of the Th2 responses until 1-2 years of age.

Thus, at birth, both mother and child's immune systems are suppressed so that the fetus enters the external world without going into immunological overload. In time, through exposure to the environment, this suppressive mechanism is gradually released, the immune system develops to ensure the survival of the infant, and maturation of all other systems in the body is activated.

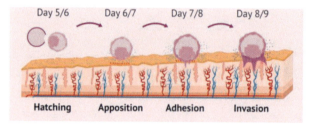

Age of maturity of the embryo at implantation

Immune Balance of Mother is Mirrored in her Childs' Immune System

A healthy immune system is a balance and interplay between the Th1 and Th2 arms of the immune system. The Th1 response is primary to Th2 response. The ratio of Th1 and Th2 responses is regulated by the DNA and is flexible and adjustable during different stages of development. This ratio is also adversely influenced by medication, immunomodulating agents, and vaccination.

Like a scale, once it loses its zero balance it no longer will make balanced immunological responses. If a mothers' immune system has been artificially tipped towards Th2 dominance, where she would have more allergic type responses, this same setting will be passed on and will set up the pathway towards increased inflammation or allergic responses in the infant.

Immune System as Interface to Other Systems in the Body

The immune system interfaces with all the major physiological systems of the body designed to ensure our survival, thus, immune system development through immunological activation effects all other systems of the body.

Development of a healthy immune system supports:

- DNA expression for self-individuation: the basis of existence

- The development of fevers and discharge pathways
- Inhibition of primitive reflexes
- Digestive function: absorption and elimination
- Neurologic function: interconnected sensation and function systems
- Intellectual discrimination: interpretation, learning, and rationale
- Personality and social development: the interface between self and society

The Benefits of Childhood Infectious Disease

Healthy immunological expression through the acute process of childhood infectious disease activates all normal stages of human development.

The struggle activated through short-lived immunological symptoms of a fever and discharge serves to activate the survival prerogative of the child.

These childhood disease expressions are an attempt for the child to immunologically differentiate itself from the immune health of the mother and generational line.

When supported this process often strengthens the child's resistance to future illnesses and sets the stage for developmental advancements in the child from infancy and childhood, through young adulthood and procreation, into complete maturation of the individual.

Natural Inhibition of Primitive Reflexes Stimulates Development

When a child leaves the self-sustaining environment of the womb, his survival is dependent on the primitive-survival reflexes built into the hind brain. These reflexes, which are automatic movements directed from the brain stem, ensure passage through the birth canal and for the first moments and initial months of life. As the infant matures the primitive reflexes gradually become inhibited. The natural inhibition of these reflexes allows for aspects of the cerebral cortex/learning function and immune system to mature.[8]

If one or more primitive reflexes remain active beyond six to twelve months of age, they are said to be aberrant. As a result, the subsequent postural reflexes, which should emerge to enable the child to crawl and walk, become delayed. Depending on the degree of delay, aspects of motor coordination, sensory perception, cognition, and/or expression will be faulty or inefficient.

Reflexes depend on visual and vestibular stimulation to become inhibited. Rocking, turning from side to side, or tonal stimulation integrates the reflexes. Shock or physical illness with excess discharge accumulating in the ears during the early months of a child's life can result in failure of specific reflexes to become inhibited, resulting in specific developmental delays.

Babies born via cesarean section, or deprived of touch, being held, and rocked, or lacking in auditory or visual stimulation will display prolonged primitive reflexes and the higher function of the brain can fail to develop.

Compression on the cranium through vaginal birth activates the survival prerogative of the infant. If there were complications in the birth process, failure to progress in labor, emergency c-section, suction or forceps, or an overly medicated birth, functionality of the neurologic systems development will mirror these effects. I.e., if there was a prolonged labor so much as to exhaust the baby, responses to life stresses later in life will mirror this failure to progress; hypoxia at birth will set the normal oxygen saturation level too low, then, when it comes time for the need of a fever the body would already be in a low oxygen state leading to the potential of febrile induced acidosis (low oxygen septicemia).

Reflexes present at birth – main function (example):

- Fear Paralysis Reflex – withdrawal and contraction (protect from danger).
- Moro reflex – rapid inhalation (first breath in life)
- Palmer reflex-gripping of hands (necessary for primates to cling to mother).
- Asymmetrical Tonic Neck reflex – as head turns baby kicks (facilitates passage through birth canal)
- Rooting reflex – head turns to side of cheek stimulation (turns to breast for nursing).
- Spinal Galant – stimulation to lumbar area causes arching away (helps with birthing).
- Tonic Labrynthine reflex – forward and backward arching of back and neck (helps with birth, coordinates breathing/swallowing-nursing).

- Symmetrical Tonic Neck reflex – arching of back with kneeling (development of crawling).
- Amphibian Reflex – stimulates the motor neurons for crawling (this is necessary to be integrated for postural reflexes to become established: for full development of cerebral cortex).

Digestive Function: Assimilation and Elimination

The digestive system is an incredibly simple system which functions through a symbiotic relationship with the biome that populates it. Its main task is intake of nutrients from the outside world, break down the nutrients and then to eliminate unusable portions and metabolic by-products. As the child matures, greater discernment between what is good for the body and what is not emerges.

In utero, the placenta delivers nutrients directly to the fetal blood system via the umbilical cord in a ready to assimilate form. Swallowing of the amniotic fluid bathes the intestinal lining with minerals and prepares it for nutritive absorption. After birth, the first nourishment an infant receives is the colostrum from mother's breast.

The intestinal lining is the organ of discernment. Healthy digestive function also leads to healthy intellectual discrimination: interpretation, learning, and rationale.

Colostrum is high in antibodies and immunoglobulins, providing the infant with the first immunological data necessary for survival. These immune factors help to stimulate various aspects of the innate immune system along with providing specific antibodies to various diseases. Oral contact with the mother's skin introduces lacto-fermenting bacteria into the infant's digestive tract which are necessary for healthy digestive function and the blood clotting mechanism. The physically intimate act of nursing ensures the appropriate emotional state necessary for parasympathetic nervous system function (digestion).

Mother's milk is amazing and has the exact necessary proportions of sugars, fats, and proteins in simple form. As the infant matures, he can process simple foods and eventually more complex foods. The elimination system works effectively to remove the waste.

Digestion starts with visual and olfactory stimulation. This in turn stimulates salivation and the release of gastric fluid. As the food passes through the alimentary canal, it is digested with the commensal bacteria. Immune cells located in the mucosal membranes of the digestive system register the relative benefit of what has been ingested. If at any point, it is perceived that the food has spoiled or is not fit for consumption, healthy immune system response would be to remove it from the body either by vomiting or diarrhea.

All these factors significantly impact childhood development and the developing immune system in both health and disease.

Social and Personality Development as a Part of the Healthy Immune System

As the immune system is differentiating self from non-self, the personality does this as well. Personalities evolve as unique expressions of individuality. Interaction with the environment forces the child to develop, interpret and respond appropriately, ultimately understanding their position in relationship to others and themselves.

In utero, the infant does not perceive any separation between itself and its environment. Birth is the first physical separation. The child remains "attached" to the mother through nursing but slowly over time begins to perceive himself as a separate being by the age of two or three.

Understanding personal boundaries, the ability to learn and take in new information, emotional regulation, and self-individuation are intricately dependent upon immune system maturation.

The healthy child exhibits a balance between right and left-brain function. The left side governs linear thinking, mathematics, and sequencing. The right side focuses upon creative endeavors and emotional responses in interpersonal relationships. These aspects of the personality, intellectual faculties, ability to learn, and emotional well-being are intricately involved with immune system response.

Following a supported infectious process whereby a fever and discharge have been allowed to follow a natural course, we often see developmental leaps in skills such as walking, talking, problem-solving **and social interaction. This fever has worked to facilitate further integration between the right and left sides of the brain.**

Children whose immune systems are occupied with incompletely resolved sicknesses, or unresolved immune responses to vaccines fail to complete this self-individuation process. Until the immune system is fully able to sort out and eliminate these pathogens, the child's personality and intellectual capacity will remain preoccupied and underdeveloped.

If children with pervasive developmental delays are supported in such a way as to stimulate more complete immune system action, maturation of their personality, intellect and social interaction will regain its natural course.

With the heat of a fever comes the purification of the body and mind much like the phoenix rising from the ashes of its ancestor.

Understanding Fevers

More often feared, many people think fevers are something to be avoided at all costs. We do know that some fevers, if left too long or if they get too high, can cause serious complications. Dehydration is one of the most common side-effects. Conversely, dehydration can also cause a fever. Convulsions can be the result of cerebral congestion from a fever that gets too high. Fevers associated with streptococcal bacteria are known to cause permanent damage to the kidneys or heart.

However, a fever that is well attended can serve a beneficial purpose. Our goal is to help you gain confidence in the workings of your child's immune system.

There are many reasons for fevers. Local or systemic bacterial and viral infections can be implicated. Heat-stroke and head injuries are also capable of producing high temperatures. Over exposure to a cold wind is a common cause. Emotional responses, such as shock or trauma, can also result in fevers. Teething children can develop a temperature with or without an apparent infection. The fever can be an important part of this developmental process.

The difference between a curative fever and a pathological one is demonstrated by the general symptoms of the person: Mood, temperament, energy, appetite, and thirst.

Fevers accompanied by restlessness, pain, agitation, listlessness, or stupor along with rapid respiration or feeble pulse are cause for concern.

Fevers left too long or too high can cause damage, i.e., increased risk of seizures or brain damage and suppressed fevers and unresolved sickness will often lead to more serious sickness: pneumonia can settle in, and the condition will relapse.

Curative Fevers

A beneficial fever will come without attended suffering. The child will exhibit a level of calmness and will want to sleep and be left alone. The temperature may reach high temperatures, but it will be followed within four to ten hours with a perspiration that marks the "breaking" of that fever.

It is the level of suffering rather than the intensity of heat that indicates what supportive measures are needed.

Intense pain, vomiting, delirium, or excess lethargy indicates the need for consulting a practitioner for homeopathic remedies to ensure a sufficiently curative fever.

Managing Fevers

It is important to monitor fevers. The concept of a curative fever must not be confused with letting a fever run wild or an insufficient fever. If left on their own, high fevers can be potentially life-threatening while insufficient fevers can become septic.

Conventional treatment is to control fevers with antipyretics. Homeopathic remedies assist the body to develop the appropriate immune response to facilitate passage from one step to the next.

Adjunctive Measures

- Plenty of fluid intake to reduce the risk of dehydration.
- Cool towels on the feet and hands to draw the heat out of the head.
- Tepid bathing should function as a gentle coaxing to dissipate heat from the inner core and soothe the body.

Supportive Measures

- Rest.
- Reduction in stimulation: light, noise, distracting activities.
- Gentle massage up and down the spine to stimulate the immune system.
- Calcium lactate supplementation.
- Vitamin C&D supplements.
- Acidophilus
- Bovine colostrum.
- Homeopathic cell salts.
- Herbal teas:
    - Lemon balm promotes perspiration.
    - Chamomile calms and relaxes.
    - Peppermint cools a fever.
    - Licorice enhances the effects of other herbs.

Homeopathic Fever Remedies

Homeopathic remedies work with the body to support the febrile process and resultant appropriate immune system response while reducing excess suffering. Homeopathic guidebooks for acute care can be referenced for more complete therapeutic applications

Aconite: Sudden high fevers accompanied with fear.
Belladonna: Sudden high fevers with a red face and headache.
Ferrum phosphoricum: Moderate fevers with weakness and flushed cheeks.
Gelsemium: Low fever with weakness and chills.
Pulsatilla: Fluctuating fevers and weeping.

Points to Remember:

- Complete immune function includes a fever.
- Distinguishing self from non-self is the first step in healthy immune function.
- Fevers are important for detoxing the body.
- Childhood infectious disease supports childhood development.
- Vaginal birth helps to activate primitive reflex inhibition and set the biome.
- Higher brain function develops through natural inhibition of reflexes.
- Intestinal biome and digestive function play a big role in immunity and social development.
- Social development is an integral part of immune system development.

Homeoprophylaxis: The Vaccine Alternative

Immunity develops through a subtle interaction between disease agents and the innate intelligence of the body

Homeoprophylaxis (HPx): The Vaccine Alternative

Imagine a method of disease prevention that is safe, natural, and causes no tears. Imagine no preservatives, no chemicals, and no ingredients you can't pronounce. Ideally this method would also be easy to administer, effective, gentle, and would serve to exercise and educate your child's immune system in a logical way while providing life-long immunity. This is the description of homeoprophylaxis (HPx): we call this education for the immune system.

Physicians, in their original intentions to heal the sick, devote multiple years to medical training, slog through years of sleep-deprived residency, and stand witness to the devastatingly worst possible scenarios. They naturally try to avoid these outcomes. The tools they are given are directed at identifying symptoms, categorizing them into concise diagnoses, and satisfying insurance companies' reimbursement requirements with prescriptive treatment protocols. They are woefully devoid of holistic thinking and terrain theory, nor do they have the knowledge of how deeply curative homeopathic remedies can be. They are certainly frustrated and fearful as they chase down symptoms with suppressive medication, attempting to avoid illness at all costs. The prevailing activity has become running away from illness instead of listening to its voice!

It's easy to get caught up in this fervor of fear and symptom suppression by giving another fever reducer, antibiotic, or nebulizer treatment to "fix" our children. The answer is really much easier than you think. The answer is a lot simpler and far gentler than the current "war on disease" through the vaccine method. Moreover, suppression of the natural immune response merely confuses the immune system, tells it not to work when infectious disease is prevalent, and drives the infectious process deeper into the body.

Of course, not everyone will choose another answer, no matter how reasonable it seems. When short on time, patience, or understanding, it's not easy to face sickness in our children and move through the process. There may be times when we knowingly choose to turn to conventional medicine as a necessary quick fix. But there is great freedom in knowing we have a choice.

Wisdom tells us that even though vaccinations may address seventeen different diseases today, we inevitably see colds and viruses move through every season, and then what? Do we need to add more vaccines to our existing extensive vaccine schedule to cover every other disease that may come along? Resorting to suppressing symptoms with another antibiotic is a poor strategy that only helps temporarily. Bacteria become antibiotic resistant, and viruses mutate.

Here, we invite you to explore the effectiveness of homeopathy and HPx to strengthen the health of the individual to reduce disease incidence. Over time, your first-hand experience with success will gradually win over your trust in managing your and your child's health. You will come to find how the homeopathic approach offers a growing understanding of how disease can play a positive role in not only your child's development through the childhood HPx immunization program but also through the additional HPx programs developed.

If you compare and contrast the methodology of HPx and Vaccination you will find that if you take all the toxic ingredients out, give one disease as a time in a way that the immune system can process disease, the only solution would be HPx.

Homeoprophylaxis is a Subset of the Practice of Homeopathy

The theory of homeopathy is based on the 'Law of Similars.' That is, the pathogenesis of a disease process that a substance has the potential to produce, when used in potency, has the potential to heal.

Such that, for example, as coffee can produce a state of hyperactivity and insomnia, the homeopathic remedy *Coffea* can, in potency, serve to resolve hyperactivity and insomnia, and *Tuberculinum* can be used to mitigate the expression of tubercular diseases.

Theory of HPx is the same as the theory of vaccination, whereby introducing disease agents into immune system prior to exposure to that actual disease stimulates immunity and activates immune intelligence.

Both homeopathy and homeoprophylaxis use potentized substances anointed onto sugar pellets, taken by mouth, as the delivery method, for both treatment and prevention.

Theory and Method of HPx

Homeoprophylaxis satisfies the process of naturally acquired disease by providing a tiny dose of the disease, but without the risks of the disease. This is accomplished by using remedies called "nosodes."

Nosodes work to stimulate general immunity through contact with the mucous membranes. The immunity engendered is much like the immunity of naturally acquired disease. HPx is administered through the sequential dosing of a specific nosode over several months or years.

The power of HPx is in the potentization process whereby the crude disease agent is attenuated through serial dilution and succussion (forceful banging). Thus, rendering what could be potentially lethal into an agent of temperance, transformation, and evolution.

Origins of HPx

James Compton Burnett, a homeopath contemporary to the development of the smallpox and rabies vaccines, was the first doctor to forcefully warn against the dangers of vaccination and the use of material disease agents to protect against serious diseases. He believed that vaccination generated a state of disease of its own.

He postulated that if the appropriate immune system reaction was not developed from the vaccine, the effect was for the injected pathogenic material to pollute the body and result in a state of chronic disease called **vaccinosis.**

Burnett argued that vaccination, as practiced by Louis Pasteur and Edward Jenner using material doses of cowpox or rabies (as the first vaccines were) would eventually end in disaster because it was only temporary protection. It did not individualize the dose to the health of the individual and would ultimately cause long-term chronic consequences.

Burnett proposed the use of a homeopathic potency of the disease as a less harmful way to encourage an immune system response without the introduction of the actual disease material into the blood.

His use of homeopathic nosode, *Variolinum* (the nosode made from smallpox) was an early instance of homeoprophylaxis.

HPx was first documented in 1801 when Samuel Hahnemann described using *Belladonna* for the prevention of scarlet fever.[9] Since that time, homeopathy has successfully prevented and treated a variety of illnesses, including childhood diseases, epidemics, cholera and typhus, and tropical diseases.

Nosodes

Nosodes are defined by the Food and Drug Agency's Homeopathic Pharmacopoeia of the United States(HPUS) as homeopathic "attenuations" of pathological organs and/or tissues, causative agents, or disease products from infected individuals, such as discharges, excretions, and secretions.

Homeopathic Attenuation

To "attenuate" means to make something smaller or weaker. In electronics, reducing the amplification of a signal without distorting it is known as attenuation. Fevers can be attenuated or reduced by cool bathing. Viruses or bacteria can be attenuated by a variety of methods that weaken its virulence such as radiation or using only a portion of the cell wall, protein coat, or genetic material. Homeopathic nosodes, are attenuated through a careful process called "potentization."

Potentization is a method by which the original pathogen is inactivated through a series of repeated dilutions. Each dilution is followed by "succussion," or the forceful striking of the vessel containing the solution against a hard surface. With the pathogen diluted to the point of no original molecules, then having been succussed (forcefully banged against a hard surface), only its energetic frequency remains. It is no longer virulent or dangerous in any way.

All material, biological and otherwise, possesses a unique energetic signature, or frequency. Diluted preparations of disease agents have been shown to emit the same energetic frequency as the original disease agent.[10] This frequency is sufficient to stimulate general immune system function.

Because all homeopathic remedies are potentized, the original culture or specimen can be infinitely reproduced from this one original source.

Nosodes are made without additives, adjuvants (chemicals intended to increase the action of vaccines), or preservatives. Nor are they incubated on any animal or human aborted fetal tissue. Nosodes are administered orally, one at a time. By touching upon the mucus membranes of the mouth, the body's first line of defense, they stimulate the normal order of immune system function.

Each HPx Program described in this book consists of a series of nosodes and supportive remedies in different potencies. Imagine that you are teaching your immune system to appreciate classical music. The first time you hear Chopin it is a new experience and met with curiosity, but no recognition. The next exposure creates a familiar resonance and perhaps the initial interest evolves into pleasant recognition and acceptance. The vibrational frequency of homeoprophylaxis acts in much the same way. Repeated doses of the disease frequency communicate with the immune system and elicit responses towards evolution.

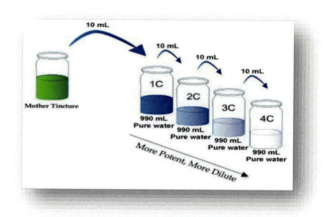

Schematic of potentization

Nosodes can be made from

- Sputum or nasal discharges
- Scrapings from mucous membranes, vesicles or cankers, pathological tissue such as cancerous tumors or tubercular encasements
- Pathological blood
- Decomposed matter
- Cultured bacteria, viruses, or vaccines

General Disease Prevention Protocols

- *Covid nosode*
- *Diphtherinum*
- *Haemophilus influenzinum*
- *Hepatitis A nosode, Hepatitis B nosode*
- *Human papillomavirus nosode*
- *Influenzinum*
- *Meningococcinum*
- *Morbillinum*
- *Parotidinum*
- *Pertussin*
- *Pneumococcinum*
- *Polio*
- *Rabies nosode*
- *Rotavirus nosode*
- *Rubella nosode*
- *Tetanotoxin*
- *Tuberculinum*
- *Varicella nosode*
- *Variolinum*

Biome Health

- *Streptococcinum*
- *Staphylococcinum*
- *Candida albicans*
- *Clostridium difficile*
- *Poly bowel*
- *Lactobacillus*

Overseas Travel

- *Choleratoxin*
- *Dengue Fever nosode*
- *Malaria Co.*
- *Malaria officinalis*
- *Typhoidinum*
- *Yellow fever nosode*

Sexually Transmitted Diseases

- *AIDS nosode*
- *Chlamydia*
- *Gardnerella vaginalis*
- *Herpes I & II*
- *Medorrhinum*
- *Syphilinum*

Inherited Conditions

- *Carcinosin*
- *Cytomegalovirus nosode*
- *Glandular fever*
- *Medorrhinum*
- *Psorinum*
- *Syphilinum*
- *Tuberculinum*

How Nosodes Stimulate Health

There are two forms of disease: acute disease and chronic disease. An acute disease is an infectious process that arises suddenly, has a rapid course of action, and spontaneously resolves. Acute disease serves as a vehicle for exercising the immune system. It can also serve as a type of vent for more chronic illness by liberating previously suppressed acute diseases (miasm) and unwanted toxins.

Chronic disease reflects the accumulation of stressors, previous unresolved acute disease and/or toxins in the body which result in deeper long-term pathology. If left to its own course, this will eventually develop into more serious illness. Think of a worker carrying a very heavy load. Over time, the burden causes his joints and muscles to weaken and become more susceptible to injury and deterioration.

Chronic disease also develops when acute disease does not fully resolve. We call this never-been-well-since or a miasmatic condition. Each acute disease, if unresolved or suppressed, will result in disease tendencies towards specific secondary or tertiary conditions related to that disease. In some instances, these tendencies can be passed onto one's offspring and will shape their health unless otherwise mitigated.

In the treatment of chronic conditions with homeopathy, especially after a nosode is administered, often an acute exonerative process is initiated. This is an action that frees the body from its burden. It can manifest as a fever, a rash, a cough, diarrhea, or other evidence of the externalization of toxins. The homeopathic nosode has successfully aroused the vital force to purge the body. This exonerative process is much like the one initiated by an acute infectious disease.

In acute disease, HPx dosing can be used before (as prevention), during (to support), or after (for complete resolution an infective process). HPx with specific nosodes can also be used to liberate inherited conditions. It does so by correcting epigenetic expression of the disease tendencies by clearing the miasmatic disposition that would create those conditions.

HPx dosing can be paired with disease specific homeopathic remedies to address the susceptibility more completely to the pathogenesis of the disease the nosode is targeting.

The administration of a homeopathic nosode can act in the same way as an acute disease. The difference between a nosode and the actual germ is that while the first is derived from the later, the effects of the energetic frequency of the germ in the body are not as violent as the actual germ.[11]

As the fever of acute disease is seen as a valve for chronic disease, the use of nosodes can act in a similar way, thus preventing the development of chronic disease.

Nosodes, when administered in the appropriate potency and dose, while stimulating immunity, act to tone an individual's health in a gentle and controlled manner.

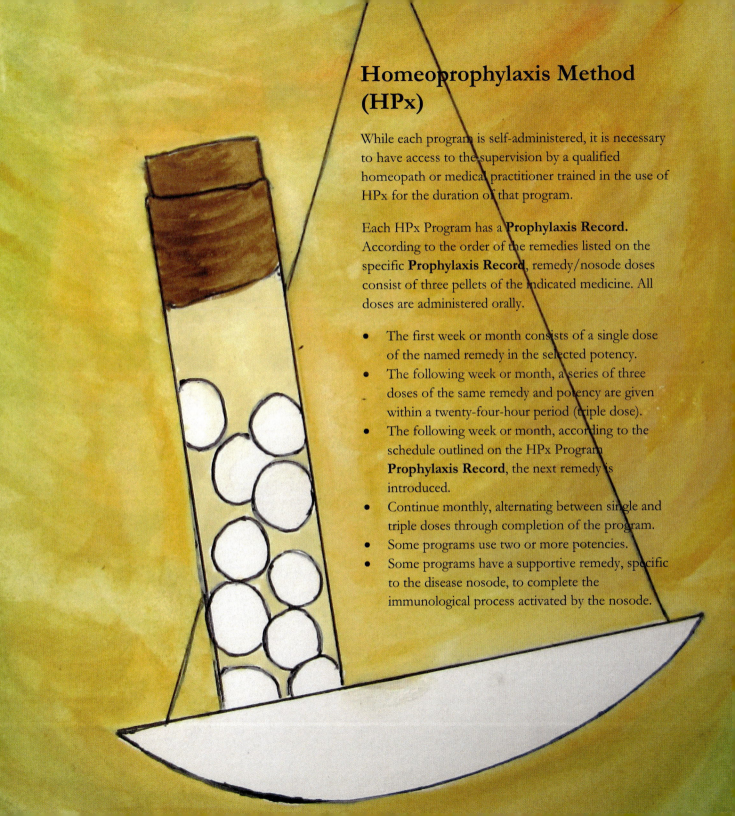

Homeoprophylaxis Method (HPx)

While each program is self-administered, it is necessary to have access to the supervision by a qualified homeopath or medical practitioner trained in the use of HPx for the duration of that program.

Each HPx Program has a **Prophylaxis Record.** According to the order of the remedies listed on the specific **Prophylaxis Record**, remedy/nosode doses consist of three pellets of the indicated medicine. All doses are administered orally.

- The first week or month consists of a single dose of the named remedy in the selected potency.
- The following week or month, a series of three doses of the same remedy and potency are given within a twenty-four-hour period (triple dose).
- The following week or month, according to the schedule outlined on the HPx Program **Prophylaxis Record**, the next remedy is introduced.
- Continue monthly, alternating between single and triple doses through completion of the program.
- Some programs use two or more potencies.
- Some programs have a supportive remedy, specific to the disease nosode, to complete the immunological process activated by the nosode.

HPx Programs for All Stages of Immune Maturation

Nosodes galvanize the immune system towards natural development, maturation, and evolution of the individual.

- Childhood diseases are meant to be contracted in childhood to capitulate aspects of childhood maturation.
- Susceptibility to certain diseases in young adults, as they are finding their way towards their independence, is based on the actual need for that disease process to measure their energy usage and claim that independence. By giving the disease in the form of a nosode these susceptibilities can be satisfied.
- Sexually transmitted diseases are intended to modify sexual behavior towards healthy sexuality in loving relationships. Nosodes of sexuality transmitted diseases will encourage this healthy self-love and interpersonal love by clearing out potential degradations of self-worth and immune health misplaced sexual energy can produce.
- Nosodes given in pregnancy can help both the mother and child clear inherited conditions.
- Nosodes given in elderly populations activate the immune system, enhance immunological memory to the infectious diseases they had early in life, to support their role as an integral member of their family.

Each HPx Program is designed to maximize the health of the recipient based on developmental maturity of the immune system and their personality and sociological functions of that age.

Every infectious disease has its own survival prerogative and innate intelligence. When administered in the right potency (homeopathic attenuation) it activates specific immunological functions for the benefit, evolution, and survival prerogative of the recipient.

Sample HPx Dosing Schedule

Dosing on Sundays	Remedy	Potency	Label	Date
1st week	Nosode	200		
2nd week	Nosode	200 triple dose		
3rd week	Supportive remedy	200		
Month 2	Nosode	1M		
2nd week	Supportive remedy	200		
Month 3	Nosode	10M triple dose		
2nd week	Supplemental Nosode	10M triple doses		

Each HPx Program schedule is created based on the following factors:

- Age of recipient using the program.
- Maturity of the immune system.
- The time needed to establish a complete immune response.
- Targeted diseases in program.
- Supportive remedies to facilitate that immune response.
- Social context of immune system function: elders, travel, sexual behavior, childhood maturation, etc.
- Risk factors verses age of recipient for the diseases.
- Developmental benefits of each disease.
- Potency is as compared to desired effect.

HPx Supervision

All HPx programs are offered under the supervision of a practitioner trained in healthy immune system function and homeoprophylaxis. An initial health profile is reviewed to determine if the Th1/Th2 ratio of the mother's or child's immune systems is within normal ranges per age of immune system maturation.

For the best results, it is expected for an individual to demonstrate healthy immune function; the ability to develop a fever and discharge prior to commencing HPx programs.

Evidence of dysbiosis or allergic responses is a sign that some constitutional homeopathic treatment may be needed before embarking on an HPx program. Prior to starting HPx previous vaccines or other immune-modulating agents may also need to be cleared from the system to normalize the Th1/Th2 ratio to receive the maximum immunological benefit from HPx.

For more details on specific HPx Programs FHCi offers or to determine if HPx is suitable for you or your child's current state of health be sure to ask your HPx Practitioner.

Potency for HPx Programs

Homeoprophylaxis can be accomplished with any potency. Lower potencies seem to be more effective the larger the group of people covered in a single prophylaxis intervention. Individual prophylaxis, or in smaller groups, higher potencies are recommended. The potencies used in the HPx Programs discussed here range from 200C, 1M, to 10M.

Full Childhood Immunological HPx Program

Sequential dosing of childhood infectious disease nosodes plays an important role in supporting, facilitating, and maintaining normal childhood development, the natural cycle of disease, and intact immune systems. HPx dosing instructs the immune system on how to make appropriate immune responses and recover.

10 (11*) diseases for a well-rounded immunological education. 200C and 10M potencies. Duration: 48 months.

As per the sample the first dose of the remedy given in the 200C potency creates a resonance with the child and initiates immune system reactivity. The triple dose of 200C the following week or month is to ensure that the resonance with that nosode is engaged on a deeper level.

The third and fourth doses in a higher potency (10M administered in a triple dose) are intended for longer and more complete fulfillment of susceptibility. Antibody production may take place with the subsequent doses. The resonance has worked to recognize of the disease, build immunity, and resultants in protection.

Whole being benefits of each nosode in the Full Childhood Immunological HPx Program

0. Disease – *Nosode*: physio-psycho-spiritual basis of the nosode.
1. Tuberculosis – *Tuberculinum*:* measuring self-preservation against ideology.
2. Polio – *Polio*: healthy intestinal lining discernment.
3. Streptococcus – *Streptococcinum*: healthy biome.
4. Diphtheria – *Diphtherinum*: activating individuality of self.
5. Whooping cough – *Pertussin*: integrating true self vs. modified self.
6. Pneumonia – *Pneumococcinum*: embodying the breath.
7. Haemophilus influenzae – *Haemophilus*: establishing personal boundaries.
8. Meningitis – *Meningococcinum*: emerging critical thinking.
9. Tetanus – *Tetanotoxin*: insulating boundaries.
10. Mumps – *Parotidinum*: formation of reproductive identity.
11. Measles – *Morbillinum*: staking one's existence in the environment.

Tuberculinum is optional. It is recommended for those individuals from South America, the Middle East, Europe, Africa, India, and Russia where either Tuberculosis is prevalent, or BCG (Tuberculosis Vaccine) is given as it tips the immune system towards Th2 responses. Even if the child did not receive this vaccine, the effects of the family heritage can be passed down and effect the Th1/Th2 ratio of the immune system.

New HPx Programs

Sequential immunological stimulation with HPx dosing plays an important role in supporting and facilitating the natural cycle of disease. Healthy immunological expression through this process activates the normal stages of human development from infancy and childhood, through young adulthood and procreation, into complete maturation of the individual. Additionally, HPx reduces susceptibility to active infectious disease resulting in less chronic disease. HPx can be applied for a variety of diverse needs to facilitate and ensure healthy immunological development, optimum resilience, and corrective cellular immunity.

Dosing with HPx nosodes offers the body an opportunity to contemplate the physical manifestations of a disease process through mild short-lived fevers, localizations, and elimination routes. In addition, the action of stress, adaptation, and resultant strengthening of the system catalyzes far-reaching planes of human development and consciousness.

The following programs have been developed and sequenced in relation to age and needs of the participant. They are measured against the nature of the immune system, the natural cycle of disease processes, the relationships of diseases to each other, and their associated remedies.

Each program follows a set schedule. In some programs nosodes are accompanied by the best supportive remedy to complete that immunological process.

Access to each program is offered under the patronship model of Free and Healthy Children International (FHCi).

Healthy Biome HPx

A healthy biome establishes the foundation of life and the vital functionality of every system of the body.

Bacteria and viruses help to maintain healthy skin and all mucosal linings, fortifying their primary purpose of interfacing with the environment. Use this program for establishing the foundation of life and vitality.

9 nosodes, 1M potencies. Duration: 9 or 18 weeks. Suitable for all age groups to correct and prevent biome imbalances.

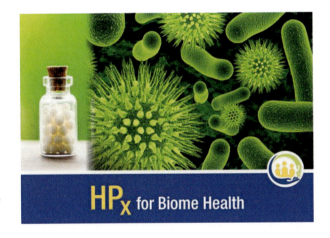

HP_x for Biome Health

Young Adult and College Prep HPx

With HPx, the action of immune stimulation, adaptation, and rest results in a strengthening of the system that catalyzes far-reaching planes of human development and consciousness. This HPx program is set for a time when emergence of the true self, social intelligence, and critical thinking corresponds with immune system maturation.

HPx dosing and resultant immune responses facilitates and supports the process of individuation of the young adult. Use this program for a robust immune system during the development and social context of college aged young adults

6 diseases and 6 supportive remedies. 200C and 10M potencies.

Travel HPx

The introduction of disease nosodes from foreign environments builds the adaptation skills necessary for those environments to expand one's immune capacity and world view.

Use this program for individuals wishing to travel to foreign countries. Particularly those countries with tropical, insect borne, and food borne diseases.

5 nosodes and 5 supportive remedies. 200C and 10M potencies. 10, 15 weeks, or longer. Suitable for all ages.

Healthy Sexuality and Pre-Procreation HPx

Sequential dosing of sexually transmitted disease nosodes for promoting healthy intimacy, tempering susceptibility to sexually transmitted diseases, and activating corrective immunity and alignment towards the divine order of creation. Use this program to promote healthy intimacy and sexuality.

7 diseases and 7 supportive remedies. 200C and 10M potencies. Recommended for couples and sexually mature individuals between the ages of 16-35 years. Duration: 7 or 14 months.

Healthy Pregnancy and Fetal Development HPx

Unless modified, inherited conditions affect the epigenetics of our children. Gestation is a transformational time for mother and fetus. By clearing any disease tendencies during pregnancy, increased health for mother and fetus is more likely. This HPx Program targets the release of inherited afflictions for optimal health in pregnancy and the liberation of your offspring. The program can be started any time prior to conception through gestation. Use this program to enhance both the health of the mother and child.

7 diseases and 7 supportive remedies for freeing both mother and child. 1M and 200C. Duration: 7 months.

Immune Health for Elders HPx

Activating the immune system memory supports the role of elders in community and family settings. Normally a grandparent's exposure to childhood diseases through interacting with their extended family activates immune memory and ensures a robust immune system within the family structure. Use this to program to stimulate these immunological memories, especially if exposure to active childhood disease is not an option.

6 diseases and 6 supporting remedies. 1M potencies. Suitable for adults 55 years and older. Duration: 6 months.

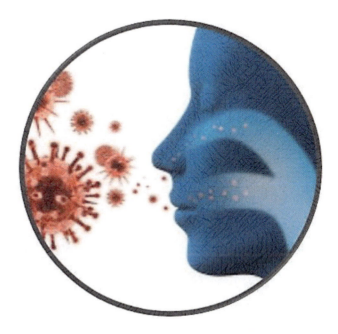

Disease agents contacting the mucus membranes

Natural disease exposure is through contact with the mucus membranes. This sets up the immunological process to activate an elimination route for resolution. HPx nosodes, taken orally, initiate this same immunological pathway. This is how true immunity is generated.

Benefits of HPx Programs

The process of homeoprophylaxis may be started at any age. The **Full Childhood Immunological HPx Program** is designed to begin at one week of age but can be initiated at any time. It is suggested that the whole family take the childhood program together to capture the benefit of herd immunological process.

The additional HPx programs, designed for various stages of life or immunological maturity, have flexible start times based on need. However, if one were to undertake HPx for life, by journeying through each program, your health and wellbeing would gain maximum immunological benefit in addition to an increased sense of sovereignty of one's existence. Thus, the ability to freely employ its body for the higher purposes of its existence will be realized.

As these programs are new, and under research, it is too early to say, but knowing the power of homeopathy and the healing potential of nosodes, we can expect there to be a reduction in many different disease potentials in the recipients.

Because HPx programs are self-administered, they are incredibly flexible. Adjustments can be made to family schedules, seasonal needs, or other variables. The **Prophylaxis Records** can be modified to include other diseases such as Rubella for pre-procreation, Hepatitis A if traveling, or if other diseases become endemic.

After the first few months of use, you will begin to witness the maturation process of you or your child's immune system in a logical way. Usually remedy responses are mild and short lived (such as fever, cough, eruptions, sweat, or restlessness for 24 hours or less). Confidence deepens as you see participants move through the circular stages of naturally contracted illnesses and begin to exhibit more vibrant health.

Fear of disease begins to fade in the presence of a new awareness that health is in motion – the act of moving in and out of illness is the exercise of building immunological maturity.

If an HPx response lasts more than a few days, contact your HPx Practitioner. They may advise you to administer a dose of the same remedy to complete its action. Occasionally the participant may be sick at the appointed time of the HPx dose. In this event, wait until three days after the sickness has resolved, then proceed with administering the next remedy on schedule.

Responses to HPx nosodes are a good sign and indicate that there is some affinity of the person's health to the remedy given. These responses are not considered side-effects, but rather the desired effect and indicate that they are stimulating a healthy immune system response to the frequency of that disease.

Conclusions

The current disease prevention and treatment methods of antibiotics and vaccinations, aimed at destroying the pathogens, denial of the benefits of the disease process, and introduction of immunomodulating substances have failed to recognize that pathogens play a necessary and important role in the evolution of humans.

If we instead view acute disease as a part of the natural selection process towards health in individuals and a vehicle for evolution in populations, shouldn't treatment and prevention be aimed at understanding the need for this dynamic relationship? Accordingly, collectively, we need a medical model that must more effectively strengthen the individual's ability to undertake this evolutionary process.

Homeoprophylaxis and vaccination share similar goals of stimulating an immune response prior to exposure. This is where the similarities end. Their methods of production and administration are vastly different. Vaccination has relied upon an attenuation model that still contains the original pathogen and has slowly added more and more preservatives, toxins, adjuvants, and antibiotics to the final product in the hopes to bolster and suppress specific aspects of the immune system at the expense of other necessary immunological processes.

These chemicals injected into the developing bodies of infants, young children, and adults alike are taking a toll on the health of humanity, making them more susceptible to chronic illnesses (see **Discussions on Vaccination** for more information).

HPx supports the developing immune system in such a way as to enhance long-term health outcomes. This result goes beyond the prevention of disease. The body's ability to mount an appropriate response and strengthen natural immunity is reflected in fewer episodes of other illnesses such as colds, allergies, and middle ear inflammation. Neurological and emotional development and maturation also occurs. This has been shown through clinical studies outlined in the chapter on **Clinical Findings**.[12, 13]

Giving a single disease nosode, one at a time, introduces the disease agent at a vibrational level that encourages a healthy immune response in the most natural way. Time is allowed for the body to assimilate and resolve one illness at a time in a way that mimics naturally acquired protection. Given by mouth, contact with the mucus membranes of the gastrointestinal tract, where immune cells do their initial work, activates the immune system.

Most importantly, homeoprophylaxis can be safely administered to children of any age, pregnant women, young adults, or the weak and elderly without risk. There is no chance of possible reaction to adjuvants or additives as there are none included. Also, as bacteria or viruses change and adapt to environmental differences over time, so will individuals who receive homeoprophylaxis, thus we will be living in harmony with these life forms while maintaining good health.

When thinking about our health, does it seem reasonable that this method may satisfy your need to protect yourself and your children?

The far-reaching effects of HPx applied to all age groups has the ability to radically transform the health of humanity.

Getting real with the health of humanity requires a reality shift. The information presented herein can help that happen.

Points to Remember:

- Nosodes do not contain chemicals or additives.
- Nosodes stimulate general immune system responses to a specific disease (fever, localization, and discharge).
- Responses to nosodes may include short-lived fevers, cough, runny nose, restlessness, sleepiness, changes in appetite or stool, or perspiration.
- Over time with repeated dosing, the general immune system (cell-mediated immunity) can trigger the specific immune system which may in turn produce antibodies. This is not guaranteed but is possible.
- If all levels of the immune system have been educated towards a complete immunological response, subsequent exposure to that disease will not result in sickness.
- There are no side-effects to the use of nosodes for homeoprophylaxis, only the desired effect of a temporary mild immune system response demonstrating the appropriate immune system function.
- Nosodes can be used before, during and after an acute disease episode.
- Nosodes can clear underlying or inherited health conditions and prevent disease tendencies from developing.
- As viruses or bacteria continue to change and adapt, humans are free to do so as well.

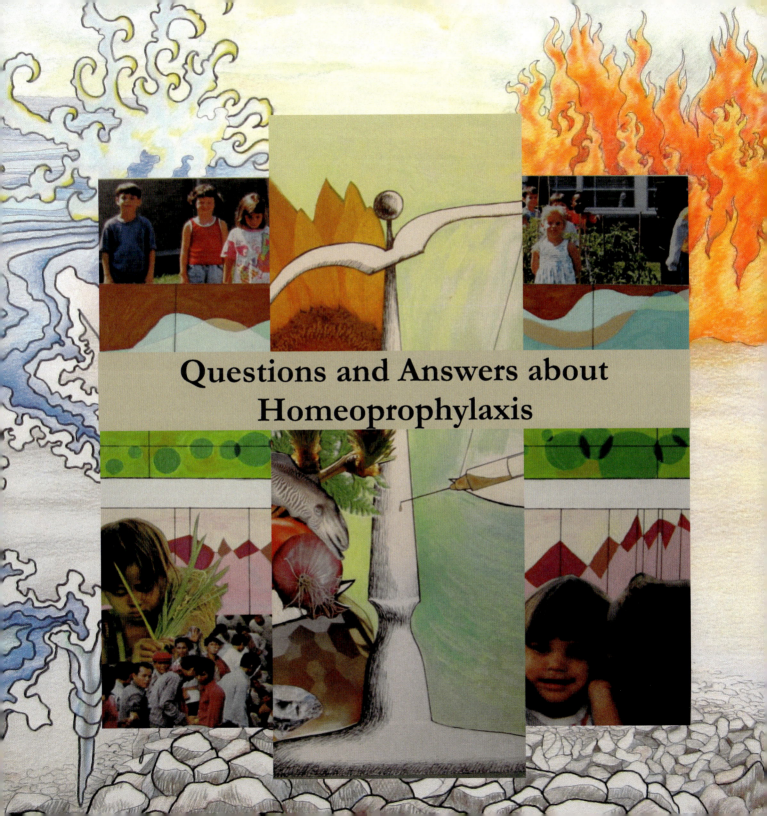

Questions and Answers about Homeoprophylaxis

It is the natural human state to inquire, weigh, and measure differences

Q-1: According to homeopathic philosophy don't you need a set of symptoms to match a remedy to for it to work? What is the justification for use of the nosode in homeoprophylaxis?

A-1: You are correct, in the practice of homeopathy, according to the 'Law of Similars,' we would need a symptom presentation to justify the use of a remedy. In homeopathic practice, we are treating a condition with a substance that produces the same condition in a healthy person, whether it be a nosode or a remedy from a plant, mineral, or animal source. Homeoprophylaxis, however, operates on a different philosophy.

– First we are dealing with 'dissimilar' diseases as opposed to similar diseases (in some of the cases) and our goal is to activate an immune response for the purpose of generating immunity.
– Secondly, we are working with pathogens that have a historical relationship to humans as we have evolved together over time and the immune system responses generated capture the benefits of this relationship.
– Thirdly, instead of working to treat an existing condition (as with homeopathic treatment) we are attempting to provide the individual with information prior to exposure to disease, so that upon exposure they would be able to respond more quickly and effectively to the disease in question. This is the same philosophy behind vaccination but without the additives, toxins, poisons, and pathological particles.
–Finally, the immune system response generated from HPx activates the benefit of that infectious disease.

Q-2: What is the difference between using a nosode of a certain disease verses the specific remedy for that disease?

A-2: If someone has already been exposed to a disease the process of disease must go on. Giving a nosode at this time will help facilitate this process. If at any point in the progress of the disease the level of suffering is too high, then it is possible to select a homeopathic remedy for these symptoms, i.e., *Eupatorium perfoliatum* would be the best remedy to treat dengue fever, *Pulsatilla* is very beneficial in the treatment of measles. The remedy would facilitate more rapid resolution of the disease. The nosode may act in a similar way, i.e., to help resolve the disease, but it is possible to individualize a particular remedy based on their symptom expression. Nosodes and supportive remedies can be used sequentially to maximize the effect.

Q-3: I heard it is possible to prevent disease with other remedies beside nosodes, like *Hypericum* or *Ledum* for tetanus. In older versions of the childhood program all the diseases were addressed with nosodes except for *Lathyrus sativus* for polio? My thinking is with titers, I understand that the body may get protection but without the nosode how will the body recognize "polio" from *Lathyrus sativus*?* *

A-3: What is best, fulfilling the susceptibility with a similar remedy to the disease or using the nosode to try to develop titers? Disease comes into the body due to susceptibility. If that is the case, the remedy which best matches the susceptibility would be best to prevent disease. Historically *Lathyrus sativus* has worked so well in the prevention of polio it was used in the childhood program.

* Please note that earlier version of this book indicated *Lathyrus sativus* was listed for polio prevention. Even though historically *Lathyrus sativus* has demonstrated exemplary efficacy towards the prevention of polio we have determined that the vaccine paradigm has propagated on the fear that polio inflicts. In our attempts to reduce that fear we have exchanged *Polio nosode* for *Lathyrus sativus* to address the energy of this fear.

** In the 13 years since the publication of the first edition of the book we have also come to understand the beneficial impact of Polio on the tight junctions of the intestinal lining which in turn enhances immunological function of the immune system.[14] It is for these reasons is has been moved into first position in the **Full Childhood Immunological HPx Program**. Polio nosode is also added into the **Healthy Biome HPx Program**.

Q-4: Also, Hypericum and Ledum are good for tetanus, just as Euphrasia is best for measles, and Phosphorus for hepatitis A. So why not use these in the program instead of nosodes?

A-4: It has to do with marketability and the common mind set on diseases and trying best to emulate the vaccine schedules and to provide a product that does not have the same risks as vaccines. Sticking to nosodes doesn't have so much to do with homeopathy, nor is it necessarily the best approach. But research has demonstrated nosodes can stimulate antibody production.

But the question is, is the production of antibodies synonymous to being immune?

This is a gray area. However as there is a variation in people's susceptibility, for instance, with measles, as *Euphrasia* will not work for everyone, it is better to go with the nosode *Morbillinum* in a program where we are trying to cover as many people as possible.

Q-5: Why do you use 200C, 1M, and 10 M potencies? Other resources often list a potency of 30C for homeoprophylaxis.

A-5: Our understanding is that higher potencies work deeper in the system. Some practitioners are fearful to use a 10M in the homeopathic treatment of cases as it can cause a homeopathic aggravation. This is not the same in HPx. 10M goes deeper and gives more lasting immunity.

The protocol we started with is from Dr. Golden and he finds this the best way. The research of FHCi confirms this. Also, for the average consumer, as the 30C is the potency available over the counter it is what gets recommended. However, if there is supervision and the person has already been exposed to the 200C, 1M, then the 10M potency will just deepen the work.

As you will find from the research listed in the next chapter however, high levels of efficacy in disease prevention in large populations can be achieved using single doses of the 30C potency. In these situations, the morphogenetic field effect of simultaneous prophylaxis in a large group of people compounds the efficacy of the single dose.

Q-6: Can this schedule be of use for a two-year old? He has not been vaccinated and I would like to know if this program would work based on the age the doses should be given according to the Prophylaxis Record? At his age, would the same doses be sufficient? Or is it based on weight and a 2 ear-old weighs more than a 1-month-old infant?

A-6: Dosing in homeopathy does not relate to the weight of the individual taking the remedy. The indicated potency number refers to the level of dilution and resultant frequency.

One dose is three pellets or several pellets given over a short amount of time (less than 24 hours). With the use of potentized nosodes, as with Homeoprophylaxis, in this energetic form there are no longer any original particles in the preparation, just the imprint of the frequency of the substance rather than a quantity of material. This frequency can be detected by the human body and after successive dosing the immune system becomes educated towards that particular disease process.

The **Prophylaxis Record** refers to a weekly or monthly time of dosing, however it could be the first week or month of age when the program is started, or the first month when the first dose is given regardless of age.

The dose is the same for an infant as it is for a two-year-old, or for a thirty-year-old. The amount of repetition is the same. Infants' immune systems, by design, are not ready to create the disease specific antibodies for the first year of life or so, however the energetic imprint of the nosode has provided the general immune system with sufficient information to repel the disease if there is subsequent exposure. If the nursing mother takes the nosode at the same time, the infant will get the added benefit of the immunological response the mother develops and expresses through her breast milk.

Q-7: I notice that you only use 8 diseases in the HPx program. Why do you not include all the diseases in the regular vaccine schedule?*

A-7: *This Childhood program has been changed since this question was originally asked. Currently there are 10-11 diseases and we have reintroduced *Diphtherinum* and added *Streptococcinum* which is not in the childhood vaccine schedule and *Tuberculinum* is optional.

The Full Childhood Immunological HPx Program does not include nosodes for hepatitis A or B, rotavirus, influenza, varicella, rubella, or human papillomavirus (HPV) for the following reasons:

- Hepatitis A is easy to treat and prevent with good hygiene and the remedy *Phosphorus.*
- Hepatitis B is a sexually transmitted disease, or from tainted blood; in areas where incidence is less than 2% of the population the WHO does not recommend Hep B vaccine (US incidence is less than 2%).[15]

- Rotavirus is easy to treat with *Arsenicum album* or *Podophyllum.*
- *Influenzinum* can be added seasonally if needed.
- It is better for children to be exposed to wild virus chickenpox for its benefits to the immune system.
- *Rubella nosode* should be used when girls reach childbearing years in a separate program. It is included in the **Healthy Sexuality and Pre-Procreation HPx Program** for the exact reason to capture the benefits of the corrective immunity *Rubella nosode* offers.
- Human papillomavirus is present in sexually active populations. This nosode may be used in a separate program. However, it is understood in homeopathic philosophy that the susceptibility to developing cervical cancer after exposure to HPV is a quality of the person rather than the direct result of the virus. Thus, it is this propensity towards cancer which must be treated rather than a specific HPx program designed to prevent HPV.
- The susceptibility to contracting HPV falls under the Miasm covered by Medorrhinum offered in the **Healthy Sexuality and Pre-Procreation HPx Program**.
- *Covid nosode* can be added if desired.

Q-8: If supplemental nosodes are added to the Childhood HPx kit, is there any particular order they should be added?

A-8: Parents can add a variety of remedies at a variety of times according to the apparent need for that remedy, age of child, and how far along they are in the program. On the **Prophylaxis Record**, there are a few months between the series of 200C doses and the first series of 10M doses. Supplemental nosodes can be incorporated then and can push out the beginning of the 10M series.

Alternatively, research in Colombia, South America, has demonstrated that dosing dates can be altered where subsequent doses can be taken as soon as two weeks after the first, starting with the 200C series. In this way, the time to go through the whole program is sped up as well and many more nosodes could be added if they seem warranted. Just make sure to note on the **Prophylaxis Record** where the supplemental remedies are added and date accordingly.

The stated order of the **Full Childhood Immunological HPx program** is such that those diseases that are of the most risk are given earlier in the program. Various other needs can influence when the supplemental nosodes are added. They can be placed in the middle of the program if there is an increase in disease incidence of that disease or if there are seasonal considerations. I.e., *Influenzinum* can be taken one month prior to fall. In other countries, where disease incidence is higher for other diseases, those remedies can be started earlier or added in earlier too, i.e., *Typhoidinum* before the rains, *Rotavirus nosode* in infants in highly populated areas with possible sewer/water

contamination, *Hepatitis A* nosode for those children in larger daycares or exposure to unsafe food, etc.

Q-9: What are the required vaccinations for overseas travel and are there homeopathic alternatives?

A-9: As far as required vaccines you must check with the CDC. So far homeoprophylaxis is not recognized at a state, federal, or international level. However, the only required vaccine for re-entry into the U.S. is yellow fever if you are returning from a yellow fever endemic area. Unless you are in a program that requires other vaccines, you can create your own prophylaxis protocol based on where you are going and the actual disease incidence. See the Tropical Disease section in the **Quick Guide** for remedy suggestions and consult a homeopath to develop a specific program for your travel needs. The **Travel HPx Program** can be used here.

Q-10: I already take probiotics, is there additional benefit from taking the Healthy Biome HPx Program?

A-10: This program is designed to regulate the tight junctions of the intestinal lining, facilitate the population of healthy bacteria, down regulate Candida and dispel pathogenic bacteria.

As HPx works at an energetic level that changes the terrain of the individual, is it changing the terrain so the bacteria introduced via probiotics can take hold. If there has been a history of antibiotics, or previous dysbiosis this program can set the stage to ensure that commensal bacteria take up residence.

Infants born to mothers with biome issues or if antibiotics are given at birth this program can help set the biome of the infant prior to starting the **Full Childhood Immunological HPx Program.**

Q-11: Does Homeoprophylaxis for sure stimulate the production of antibodies?

A-11: Research has demonstrated that in similar programs (Colombia, South America) children at three years of age have developed titers after commencing the program at infancy. However, we do not know if it takes three years of the program to develop the titers or if it takes until three years of age for the immune system to develop the titers.

Before we can answer this question completely, we must review the misconceptions of the vaccine paradigm. The basis of the vaccine paradigm is the quest to make antibodies. Research shows that some vaccines, when given repeatedly, will force the body to make antibodies in most people. The standard of the vaccine industry assumes that if antibodies are produced, then there is immunity. But is this really true? And is this the standard to be held to? I.e., it is assumed that if you have been vaccinated you have antibodies. The litmus test in this paradigm is for the un-vaccinated to prove antibodies to avoid vaccines. Truth is, however, many who have been vaccinated do not make antibodies. But, in the eyes of the officials, if they had the vaccine that is enough proof for them. There are also those that make excessive antibodies from vaccines, like an allergic reaction, the result of which is a system in a heightened allergic state causing a myriad of other inflammatory symptoms.

In attempts to make vaccines 'safer,' in 2000, the amount of antigen in a single vaccine had been reduced. To ensure that the immune system makes a sufficient response, high amounts of aluminum or aluminum salts have been added to force an allergic reaction to the antigen, i.e., antibodies. We know that one dose of vaccine does not always produce an antibody response and so more doses have been added to the vaccine schedule to make up for this inadequacy. The more doses added to the schedule, the more allergic conditions that arise because of this repetitive immunological stimulation.

The antibodies generated from a vaccine are short-lived, allergic responses to disease, not full immunity. This means you can still contract the disease because you have only developed a one-sided antibody response to the antigen, not a full response to the disease process that would involve

the general immune system and a cell-mediated immune response.

Natural disease is the only way to produce life-long immunity and life-long antibodies. Natural immunity is developed through full engagement of both the general and specific branches of the immune system. General immune system function is initiated with contact on the mucous membranes by an antigen. As the antigen passes the mucous membranes, specific immune function is stimulated, so that antibodies are made to disable and discharge the antigen. A balanced immunological response is a state of both an adequate febrile response and localization – which are the actions of the general immune system to reconcile infections (Th1); plus, having an adequate tolerance to ward off excessive inflammation, allergic responses, and autoimmune conditions (Th2).

It is the capability of the body to resist harmful microorganisms or viruses from entering it that is the best form of immunity. Can vaccines accomplish this if they are injected, therefore bypassing the peripheral immunological markers, which need to be engaged before a systemic antibody response is generated?

If the surface membranes are sufficiently stimulated towards an infectious agent, it is possible to garner general immunity to a disease without antibodies being produced. This is what homeoprophylaxis (HPx) does.

HPx doses are taken orally, touching upon the mucous membranes, calling upon the body to produce a general immune system reaction to the disease entity. This general immune system response is like a mini rehearsal of the disease elimination process. If this response is sufficient, it will engender immunity without the need for antibodies to develop.

HPx is the use of homeopathically prepared disease entities, (a.k.a Nosodes). The original disease source, either a cultured pathogen, sputum, or discharge from an infected individual, is potentized through a series of dilutions and succussions to arrive at an alcohol solution holding the energetic memory of the disease entity and therefore information about the normal immunological response to that entity (in the case of nosodes sourced from human discharges). The potentized dilution is applied to sugar pellets, the alcohol evaporates and only the information about the disease entity remains. When given orally this energetic information activates a general immune system response. As there is no antigen present (due to the dilution process) no antigen enters the blood, thus negating the need for the development of antibodies to disable and eliminate the antigen.

Therefore, HPx stimulates immunity without the need for antibodies. This is not to say however that in some instances HPx does not produce antibodies, or even if antibodies are the true test of immunity.

The unfortunate meaning of this is that if we are trying to satisfy the rationale of the illogical vaccine paradigms' need for antibodies, we may not be able to do so with HPx. But certainly, we can reduce susceptibility to contracting disease and gain the immunological benefits of the disease through the process.

With the use of HPx, immune systems become stronger and more able to navigate through an infectious disease process as they have been sufficiently educated to do so.

Q-12: Will the antibodies show in a titer test? Sometimes these are accepted as proof of immunization from the required vaccines for school.

A-12: Most schools will accept a waiver to vaccines based on state law and vaccine exemptions and they are not concerned with titers. Some states have removed philosophical exemptions. It is up to parents and vested individuals to stand up for your rights to protect yourself and your children from state mandated vaccine regimes.

Q-13: If I give these nosodes to my child then will he get the infection from the HPx or just a milder case? If he develops symptoms, is he contagious?

A-13: With regards to the response to an HPx nosode, given as prophylaxis for a specific disease, we are exposing a child to an attenuated pathogen, much like that in a vaccine. However, the method of attenuation is such that the pathogen is completely diluted out of the solution. All that remains is the memory and frequency of the pathogen. This memory is sufficient to stimulate an immune system response in the peripheral immune system, as if the child has been exposed to the actual pathogen. The child will not get the actual disease, as there are no pathogens in the nosodes, but rather only the energetic imprint stimulates the immune system to behave as if it has the disease for a short time (usually 12-24 hours) in a very mild way.

Correspondingly as there is no pathogen in the nosode shedding will not occur and the individual is not contagious.

Q-14: I am considering using homeoprophylaxis with my newborn but only for the first two years of her life and then switching to traditional vaccines. How would that work? Is it even possible?

A-14: This question makes me think of more questions. I understand the reason to postpone vaccinations until a child's immune system is more mature to be able to properly respond to the vaccines. Following that line of reasoning, it would also make sense to postpone the schedule and give one vaccine at a time, waiting between doses to be sure the immune system had fully responded to and recovered from the previous vaccine. Some diseases have more potential to be life threatening in infants, such as diphtheria, whooping cough, pneumonia, meningitis, etc., and that is why they are in infant vaccine schedules. As the child gets older, they are less susceptible to complications from those diseases. With this in mind, if one were to postpone the vaccines until the child is older, then why vaccinate at all if they have passed the critical time?

Following this line of thinking for homeoprophylaxis, the aim would be to help to protect the infant in those early years with a far less toxic method than vaccination; to stimulate the child's immune system without causing any negative side-effects or damage.

Why at two years of age start the regular vaccines? If the homeoprophylaxis works as it is supposed to, then to continue and finish the repeated dosing ought to be sufficient to complete the immune system response. While the first dosing of the HPx is sufficient in providing short-term protection, repeated dosing over the next years is needed to provide lasting immunity.

Switching to vaccinations at this time would not really allow the full benefit of the HPx and you would still get negative vaccine responses with their aluminum adjuvants, thimerosal, and incomplete disease expression side-effects.

Q-15: I know I don't want to introduce vaccines to my newborn and as much as I know I can protect her through breastfeeding at this stage, I am not sure how much I truly believe homeoprophylaxis will protect her as much as traditional vaccines in the future. If so, what would be the best potency to use with the homeoprophylaxis if I plan to vaccinate in the future?

A-15: Before addressing this, we must understand the meaning of protected. As described in many previous sections of the book the process of developing immunity is a complex process. Both the general and specific aspects of the immune systems need to be fully engaged, to develop a fever, localization and discharge, and subsequent antibodies.

Also, if the mother did not contract the diseases naturally in childhood, she will not be passing on protective antibodies to her infant. In the case of most naturally contracted childhood diseases, once resolved, the process protects the mother for life and the future child during the first year of life. She would then be passing on antibodies through breast feeding.

Vaccines and HPx both attempt protection from infectious disease through modified contagion.

Vaccines are artificially denatured and are attenuated by incubation on foreign mediums which may corrupt the disease matter with toxic foreign substances, while HPx nosodes are attenuated through dilution. Accordingly, the energetic signature of original disease matter remains intact.

Please refer to **Q-11** for a more complete answer to the antibody responses generated.

As for potency, the question remains as to which is best, and which will for sure produce antibodies. Golden used to give ascending potencies, i.e., 30C, 200C, 1M, 10M, and then repeat this series several times. After a time, he switched to the existing protocol of 200C then 10M doses repeated three times. We have adopted this method.

It depends on the health of the person and availability of the remedy and how knowledgeable the person is about usage. Usually, the 30C is self-administered while 1M is through a practitioner. The 1M would last longer and go deeper into the immune system.

Contraction of childhood diseases by the mother in childhood is the best protection for her infant in the first months of their life.

We hope that after reading this book you will find that HPx is the safer, more rational approach to immune education which results in disease protection.

Q-16: My child has been previously vaccinated but has not done the complete vaccine series, how do I know if I need to do more vaccines or if I can switch to HPx, and do I need to do all the nosodes in the kit if they have already had those vaccines?

A-16: To find out if your child has developed antibodies to a particular disease in a vaccine you can go to your local doctor and have a blood antibody titer drawn. Also, keep in mind that it takes several doses of a vaccine to stimulate antibody production and it also takes your child to be several years old before they can make antibodies. Also, that over time previous antibody development will wane from vaccines. Finally, antibody production is not necessarily equivalent to immunity.

As for how this program is set up in order to keep it within the confines of continued research, all children are advised to take all the remedies in the program, even if there has been previous vaccination. Taking the nosodes will help to stimulate a more complete immune response than the vaccines did.

The other benefit of the program in its entirety is that we are embarking on stimulating the immune system in a multifaceted way. With this there is the potential to have the benefit of evolutionary aspect each disease nosode offers. Research has demonstrated that use of nosodes in this way improves the overall level of health of the child.

Q-17: After a vaccine, we develop antibodies. If we detox a previous virus or vaccine with homeopathic treatment, do we lose the antibodies as well?

A-17: Truth is 'detox' is the wrong word for the process. There are various mechanisms at play with vaccines:

1. They can create an imbalance in the immune system with heightened antibody production paired with heightened allergies, and behavioral conditions. This has more to do with the aluminum. Detox relates to balancing the excessive histamine response in the immune system generated by the aluminum.

2. If antipyretics were used at the time of vaccination the disease is driven deeper into the body as the purpose of the fever is to activate the discharge route. Without elimination, there would be continual antibody production but the immune system never eliminates it: I.e., measles virus settles into the mucosa of the gut which then is released intermittently for years after the vaccine without active disease. Here detox refers to helping the immune system fully remove the measles virus.

3. The immune system becomes overwhelmed with the excessive white blood cell response causing mini strokes in the fine capillary beds of the circulatory system. This requires different remedies than those used to balance the immune system. It is not detox at all but rather remedies to help with tissue repair in those damaged areas.

4. To clear the vaccines the body localizes the antigen/antibody complex to the ears. This gets misdiagnosed as an 'ear infection.' Too many 'ear infections', are treated with too many antibiotics so that now we have an excess yeast situation and suppressed immune system clearing responses. In this situation, we aim to clear the yeast, then help the body learn how to get a fever and develop appropriate discharges to vent the system. This process may include another 'ear infection' and hopefully rupture of the ear drum to push the vaccine matter out, or this matter may be discharged via the stool, vomiting, or skin eruption.

5. As the immune system has become confused, it doesn't know how to eliminate the toxins in vaccines such as mercury or aluminum salt. Once the immune system is supported so that it can function better, then detox of heavy metals occurs naturally. For this condition 'detox' is the correct word.

6. At the beginning of constitutional homeopathic treatment we expect fevers to develop. The fevers may be high, or often, and will be accompanied by suffering which will need to be mitigated with remedies. Eventually, as the child gets stronger, they will be able to get the right level of fever and not get too sick. Fevers are part of the natural development of a strong immune system and are necessary for the vaccine 'detox' process.

The fevers produced will stimulate a more appropriate immune system response to the previous vaccines by supporting the desired response of appropriate antibody levels. If antipyretics or antibiotics are given at any time after a vaccine or after homeopathic treatment has begun, the whole process is thwarted and then your child will remain in one of the above situations.

The 'detox' process is more to balance the immune system response out of the allergic response and heightened antibodies to normal antibody levels. In the future, the child can get a fever and resolve a sickness in a few days with minimal support. As with all vaccines, the artificial antibody production is temporary, with elevated antibodies lasting for a few years. Then they wear off, hence the need for boosters.

Q-18: My eighteen-year-old daughter had (was forced to have) the flu vaccine two weeks ago. At two weeks to the day, she developed excruciating back pain (we now think is kidney related), ascending paralysis which included her legs, hands, and jaws 'falling asleep' (this is now ok). She also had nausea and weakness. That was six days ago. She now still has mild back pain, some nausea and weakness. What can I do for detox to prevent kidney damage, which is my main concern?

A-17: Please call a homeopath right away and go in for a consultation. The flu vaccine has made it into her spine and that is causing the ascending paralysis. Check out the CDC website for adverse events from flu vaccine. You will find these symptoms listed. Be sure to call the doctor who gave the vaccine and make sure they report this as an adverse event to the CDC. If they don't want to, you can report the event yourself to the Vaccine Adverse Events Reporting System (VAERS). Normally they only register those reactions that occur in the first twenty-four to forty-eight hours after a vaccine, but if after you go to a homeopath and they treat the condition with remedies to address ailments from the vaccine, and your daughter gets better, then you know for sure this was a vaccine adverse event.

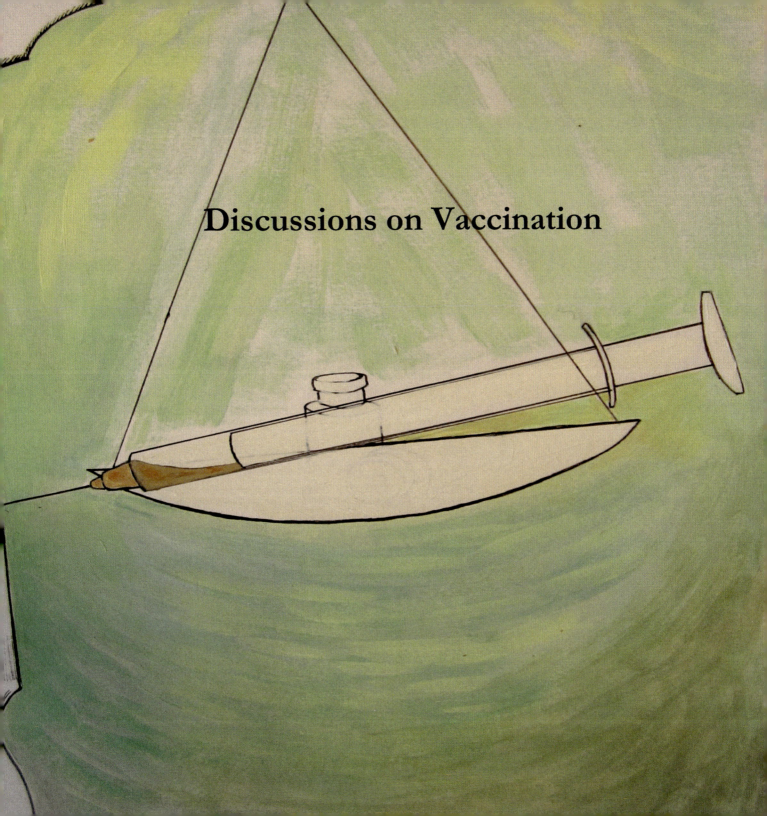

Discussions on Vaccination

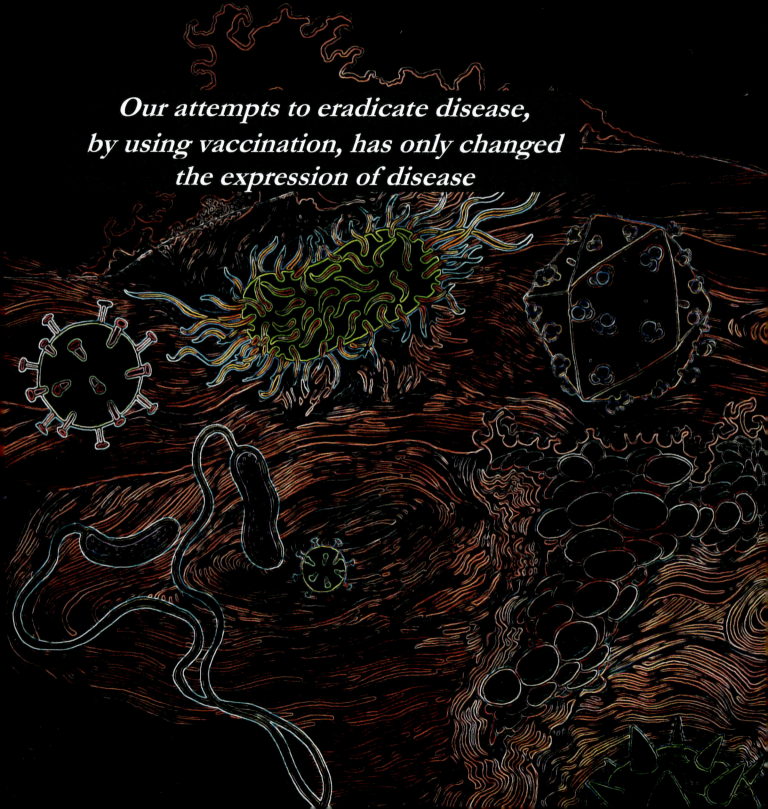

*Our attempts to eradicate disease,
by using vaccination, has only changed
the expression of disease*

Discussion on Vaccination

The World Health Organization (WHO) tells us that infectious disease incidence is directly related to inadequate nutrition, contaminated water, and poverty.[16] In the developed world the greatest reduction in infectious disease mortality has been related to public health care measures directed at alleviating these conditions.

Our fear of disease and the inability to adequately alleviate poor nutrition and contaminated water supplies places a large emphasis on the use of antimicrobials and vaccines. Many pathogens, which are evolving life forms, have become resistant, and the need for the development of costly new drugs or vaccines grows larger every day.

The prevailing paradigm is that disease is the enemy to be feared and that human beings are somehow flawed in their ability to resist illness without pharmaceutical intervention.

Some argue that if we just continue to make vaccines or develop drugs for every disease agent then we have satisfied the problem. Supporters of the vaccine model purport that if we stimulate immunity with vaccines in a large enough number of individuals, then we accomplish what is thought of as herd immunity. Herd immunity is what takes place when a certain percentage of animals within a herd acquire a natural disease and survive. Their health becomes more robust with this newly gained immunity and disease incidence goes down. The weaker animals are then protected due to the reduced disease incidence. Applied to the human population, it's thought that if enough are vaccinated, then those who cannot sustain the immunological stimulation of a vaccine will be protected from the disease due to the decreased incidence of the disease.

Since the mid-1950's, the CDC's recommended vaccination schedule[17] has skyrocketed from five vaccines – diphtheria, pertussis, tetanus (DPT), measles and polio, to seventy-two doses of multiple diseases by the age of eighteen. Additions in the past decades include MMR (live-cell vaccine), Hib, hepatitis B given at birth, varicella vaccine (live-cell vaccine), pneumococcal vaccine, meningococcal vaccine, rotavirus, hepatitis A, HPV vaccine and annual influenza and Covid vaccines beginning at six months to one year of age.

Surely the intentions of doctors and scientists were noble in protecting us from disease, but have we become short-sighted in our tolerance of the growing list of side-effects and long-term health outcomes?

We must question whether the extensive increase in the recommended schedule is playing a role in the increase of allergies, food sensitivities, pervasive developmental delays (autism) and autoimmune disorders in children.

Here we invite you to examine with us the current model of vaccination from a holistic perspective of the immune system considering understanding the function of disease.

If we are to inject multiple disease agents in an infant to elicit an immune system response, then we must be able to recognize the response we are getting and determine if it is the desired response.

66

Theory and Method of Vaccination

It is understood that injected disease material will stimulate the immune system to make antibodies. It is assumed that antibody production is synonymous with immunity.

Repeated doses are necessary to stimulate sufficient antibodies to mimic immunity. Booster shots are needed to keep antibody levels elevated. Only naturally acquired disease confers long-term protection.

Origins of Vaccination

Smallpox epidemics were rampant in Europe throughout the Middle Ages and still widespread and fatal during the late 1700's. Also, present, but a less severe form of eruptive disease, was cowpox. The observation that people previously infected with cowpox were immune to smallpox, led scientists to the idea of inoculating people with cowpox disease to prevent smallpox. This inoculation material produced a mild local inflammation and discharge like that of smallpox and in some people generated life-long immunity to smallpox.

From the works of Edward Jenner, it was this observation, in conjunction to what Louis Pasteur, and Robert Koch postulated, that the vaccination method was developed.

Scientists then researched the potential of preventing other diseases by introducing live viruses to stimulate immunity. Experiments with dogs and the rabies virus were undertaken. Unfortunately, this method killed many dogs until Louis Pasteur had the idea to incubate the virus in rabbits to lessen its virulence. This was the first attempt at attenuation, or the weakening of the virulence of a disease. The goal of vaccination was to stimulate antibody production (humoral immunity) and it was assumed that elevated antibodies were equivalent with immunity.

This method of attenuating the virus in another host species tissue is still used today in the production of vaccines.

Attenuation in Conventional Vaccines

Today live vaccines that contain weakened forms of the disease pathogen are common. Some attenuated vaccines are the BCG for tuberculosis, and vaccines for measles, mumps, chickenpox and polio.

Attenuation can be achieved by denaturing or weakening the virulence of the viral DNA/RNA or bacterial strains through heat, radiation, or genetic modification, or by incubation on a secondary live cell culture, such as aborted human fetal tissue, animal cells (pig's intestines, mouse cells, monkey's kidneys etc.), yeast, or egg mediums.

Proposed Advantages of Attenuation

- The virulence of the disease is weakened.
- Ease of administration (such as oral polio vaccine).
- IgA, IgG, and IgM antibodies may be produced.

Problems of the Vaccine Attenuation Method

- Depending on the incubation source, DNA from the live cell cultures (either foreign viral or host DNA) can combine with the viral DNA and be inadvertently maintained in the vaccine serum, i.e., HIV came from the monkey kidney cells the polio virus was incubated in;[18] other viruses have been found in rotavirus vaccine incubated in pigs' intestinal cells.[19]
- The bacterial or viral strains are still present in the final product.
- As vaccines are injected, the body's normal excretory routes have not been activated to remove them. Incompletely excreted material will gravitate to its organ of affinity, i.e., measles to the meninges or gastrointestinal tract, the neurotoxins of DTaP to the nervous system, hepatitis B to the liver, etc.
- Vaccines with human DNA, (those vaccines incubated on aborted human fetal tissue) set up an immune system response to human DNA possibly leading to autoimmune diseases, i.e., rheumatoid arthritis.

Additives

A variety of additives are included in vaccines. Detergents are added to clean the vaccine from processing. Thimerosal preservative helps to "fix" the vaccine by keeping it sterile if the vaccine is delivered in a multi-use vial. Theoretically thimerosal was removed from vaccines in the early 2000's, as such it is no longer listed on the vaccine excipient lists, however multidose vials do have small amounts of mercury to sterilize the vaccine. Antibiotics are used to eliminate other pathogens.

Additives
- Detergents/preservatives
- Formaldehyde
- 2-phenoxyethanol
- Polysorbate 80
- Thimerosal
- Antibiotics
    - Neomycin
    - Gentamicin
    - Polymyxin B
    - Streptomycin

Mercury based thimerosal is a neurotoxin. The antibiotics in vaccines can set up future allergies to those antibiotics.

Adjuvants

Adjuvants (from the Latin adjuvare meaning "to help") are the power boosters, or components to encourage the immune system to recognize and react to the antigen. They also reduce vaccine production costs due to the need for less antigen, serving as a convenience and money-saver to the pharmaceutical companies.

Adjuvants
- Aluminum, Aluminum phosphate
- Monosodium glutamate
- Oil emulsions (peanut)
- Endotoxins
- Squalene

Side-effects of the adjuvants include increased Th2 or inflammatory activity resulting in heightened allergic responses.[20] Adjuvants will increase inflammatory activity to all the ingredients in the vaccines as well as to the antigen if consumed or exposed to at a later date, i.e., peanut oil, casein, eggs, yeast, human DNA, etc.

The goal of adjuvants in vaccines is to stimulate specific antibody production by boosting Th2 function. Recent studies have shown that while certain vaccines do increase antibodies, they do it along with activation of mast cells, eosinophils causing allergic responses, all at the expense of Th1, general immune system, function such as macrophages and febrile responses.[21]

mRNA Vaccine Manufacturing

With the creation of SARS-CV2 virus, came the creation of mRNA vaccines. mRNA vaccines are made from synthetically produced mRNA strands developed through CRISPR technology. This technology allows for genome editing that give scientists the ability to change an organism's DNA and for genetic material to be added, removed, or altered at specific locations in the genome. Once the genetic sequence is established, a solution of nucleotides is exposed to the frequency of the desired genetic code and the mRNA strand self-assembles.

This is how the Covid vaccines are made. The genetic code of SARS-CV2 also holds gain of function genes. mRNA has the capacity to alter a host's DNA due to the existing relationship between RNA and DNA. This means that they have the capacity to alter the recipients genetics and immune system function. Accordingly, the long-term effects of gain of function synthetically created mRNA vaccines are untold.

While these vaccines do not have adjuvants or additives these types of vaccines require cold storage to maintain their integrity. However, as described above they have the potential to radically alter the course of humanity through altered gene expression.

Method of Administration

Vaccines are typically administered through an intra-muscular injection. This by-passes the natural route of contagion, i.e., exposure to the mucus membrane of the respiratory or gastrointestinal tracts. As a result, the immune response is not being engaged in the same way as a natural exposure.

Febrile responses and subsequent antibody responses require initial stimulation of the immune system cells located in these peripheral membranes. Injection imports pathogenic material directly into the system without any forewarning. The result is a delayed immune system response, if at all, and immune system confusion about whether this is foreign material, and if it is, what to do with it.

If the system is not given the opportunity to naturally interact with a virus or bacteria and respond with a fully orchestrated immune response, will it still be able to recognize offending agents adequately when met through more natural means?

Multiple Vaccines Given at Once

While each state in the United States has its own vaccine schedule, most states adhere to a similar schedule. Around the world similar vaccine schedules are used. The U.S. however gives the most doses of vaccines of any country in the world, thirty-six before the age of five, compared to eleven to thirteen in most European countries.

The U.S. has the highest incidence of autism and ranks 34 in infant mortality.[22] Relative autism incidence in children who are 8-years old at the time of analysis: from first edition to second edition of this book:

- In 2009: Average of one in 88; 1 in 54 for boys
- 2020: Average of one in 36; one in 23 for boys, one in 87 girls. [23]
- Highest incidence of deaths after vaccines occurring at two months of age (interestingly at the same time of the first set of vaccines).[24]

At the time of this publication hepatitis B vaccine is the first vaccine given at birth, usually in the first twenty-four hours. In other countries, this vaccine is given in combination with BCG (for Tuberculosis). In the U.S. at two months of age infants are inoculated with eight different diseases. This process is repeated at four and six or eight months. At twelve to fifteen months the process is repeated with twelve diseases at one time. The vaccine schedule repeats most vaccines again at four years, and again at fourteen years, for a total of fifty different doses of these seventeen diseases. With the recommended annual flu shots, the child has a total of seventy-two vaccine doses before age twenty.

70

Vaccines Given in Pregnancy

The naturally suppressed immune system in pregnancy tips the immune system towards Th1 response. To produce an antibody response, high amounts of aluminum are injected along with the vaccines. This aluminum tips the both the mother and infant's immune systems more towards Th2 response setting up the pathways towards allergic reactions. Additionally, aluminum is a neurotoxin. This toxin goes to the brain of the developing fetus and can produce neurological damage.

The common vaccines given in pregnancy are Influenza, TDaP (tetanus , diphtheria, whooping cough), and sometimes Covid vaccine. Each vaccine plays a different role in altering the health of both the mother and child.

Vaccines Given at Birth

The infant's immune system is naturally suppressed to not make antibodies for the first year of life. When vaccines are given at birth, such as the hepatitis B vaccine usually administered within the first 24 hours, the immune system does not respond to discharge the vaccine.

Rather, as hepatitis B is an RNA virus it can insert itself into the child's genome, the disease remains in the system, gravitates to the organ of affinity, and acts like a toxin in that organ. E.g., Hep B alters the livers' ability for normal methylation. Whooping cough toxin goes to the brain causing spasms and tics.

It normally takes a developed immune system ten to twenty-one days to completely process a naturally contracted disease entity. Is it reasonable to expect that an infant's immune system can develop an organized and appropriate immune response when the system is repeatedly inundated by multiple chemicals and disease agents?

Reflecting upon the necessary circular process of prodrome – inflammation – fever – discharge – sweat – resolution, this rapid-fire method of inoculation does not give the body sufficient time to respond in an organized fashion.

The developing immune system of an infant, by design, is incapable of developing antibodies during the first year of life and must rely upon the action of the innate immune system to remove the injected pathogenic material via a fever and discharge.

If these responses are suppressed with Tylenol or antibiotics, we have unintentionally thwarted the intended immune system response initiated by the vaccine.

Instead of strengthening the immune system and building natural immunity, the exposure to so many diseases at once, can keep the child stuck in the circular process of repeated coughs, colds, fevers, and 'ear infections.' In worst case scenarios, this will lead to pervasive developmental delays and autism.

Double-blind random controlled vaccine safety studies test single vaccines as compared to a control group of the same vaccine without the antigen, but with the same adjuvants, additives, and preservatives. The responses generated that are unique to the single vaccine are classed as the side-effects. Responses common to both groups are excluded from the results.

There has never been a study on the effects of all the vaccines in the childhood vaccine schedule.

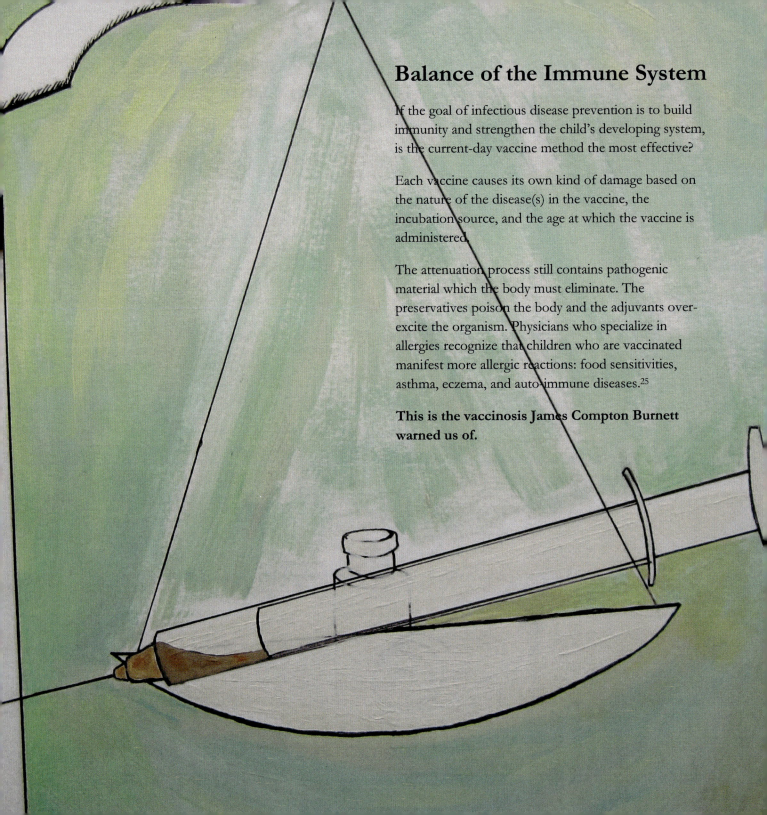

Balance of the Immune System

If the goal of infectious disease prevention is to build immunity and strengthen the child's developing system, is the current-day vaccine method the most effective?

Each vaccine causes its own kind of damage based on the nature of the disease(s) in the vaccine, the incubation source, and the age at which the vaccine is administered.

The attenuation process still contains pathogenic material which the body must eliminate. The preservatives poison the body and the adjuvants over-excite the organism. Physicians who specialize in allergies recognize that children who are vaccinated manifest more allergic reactions: food sensitivities, asthma, eczema, and auto-immune diseases.[25]

This is the vaccinosis James Compton Burnett warned us of.

Comparing and Contrasting the Method of HPx and Vaccination

Similarities

- Both aim to prevent disease.
- Both introduce a disease agent into the body with the intention to stimulate immunity prior to exposure to disease.

Differences

Vaccination
- Material dose; live, attenuated, or killed virus, bacteria, or toxin, in crude dose.
- Adjuvants to stimulate allergic response (aluminum salts).
- Other additives with the possibility of other viruses, human aborted fetal tissue and DNA, animal by-products etc.
- Preservatives such as thimerosal, formaldehyde, etc.
- Germ/adjuvants injected directly into the bloodstream by-passing peripheral immune system.
- Multiple diseases given at once.
- Specific antibody production expected in immune systems that are too immature to produce antibodies (infants until 1-2 years of age).

Homeoprophylaxis
- Energetic dose: substances are potentized/diluted to remove the material dose but retain memory of disease/pathogen.
- Nosodes are sourced from pure germ/viral culture or human discharge in response to the germ or environmental stressor.
- No adjuvants, preservatives, or contaminants.
- Administered orally with sugar pellets.
- Single disease at a time.
- From birth on, general immune system functions are active and responsive to general stimulation.

Comparing and Contrasting the Effects of HPx and Vaccination

Effects

Vaccination

- Targets specific antibody production without stimulating the general immune system. Results in delay in immune system reaction and confusion.
- Disease material is grafted upon the individual; disease is not expressed acutely but gravitates to the organ of affinity and manifests chronic symptoms, i.e., Hep B goes to the liver, MMR to the gastrointestinal or nervous system, DTaP to the nervous system, etc.
- The system may chronically liberate live viral particles.
- mRNA vaccine will alter the genetics of the recipient.
- Allergic response driven by aluminum adjuvants results in skewed Th1/Th2 immune response.
- Toxic effects of preservatives, such as mercury or aluminum poisoning, result in behavior changes, neurological deficits, etc.
- Increases susceptibility to acute and chronic disease processes; either over-reactive to all stimuli resulting in frequent illnesses, or under-reactive leading to pervasive developmental delays, etc.

Homeoprophylaxis

- Stimulates general immune system response before specific immune system response. Results in immune system processes like that of natural disease exposure.
- No disease material present to become engrafted in the individual, however specific organs of affinity become familiar with the frequency of the disease through the energetic exposure.
- Fulfills susceptibility to that acute disease; makes the person less likely to contract the disease.
- Lessens susceptibility to acute and chronic disease.
- Helps to liberate chronic disease.

Conclusions

Out hope is that now with this deeper understanding you continue to explore the subject of vaccines in the immune system. With this expanded awareness, you can discuss the issue more thoroughly with your doctors and partners to navigate your choices regarding the health of your children. Some scientists are also beginning to seriously question the methods used to produce vaccines, as well as the additional ingredients they contain such as additives, preservatives and adjuvants. They also need to look at the way they are administered via injection and the consequences of loading multiple vaccines at once into young, developing systems.

In findings from Harvard Medical school, Dr. Uldrich von Andrian recently demonstrated that a partnership between the innate and adaptive arms of the immune system is the most critical mechanism for resolving infections. This yet again calls into question the accepted theory that antibody production (Th2 response) is the main requirement for immunity.[26]

Furthermore, the work Dr. Luc Montagnier, where he discovered the infectious agents emit energetic frequencies supports the use of energetic potentized remedies for disease treatment and prevention with the understanding that all disease arises from an energetic imbalance.[27]

Effects in Individuals

Childhood vaccines are intended to stimulate humoral immunity by the adjuvant driven forced production of antibodies in infants' as their immune systems are insufficiently developed to make specific antibodies. Too many diseases are given at one time and the rate of repetition is too frequent for immature immune systems to respond effectively and completely. The resultant inflammatory state leaves disease incompletely eliminated and resolved.

Suppressed diseases, or those not adequately resolved by the system, are routed to the nervous system or other organ of affinity resulting in fevers, brain inflammation, or other organ damage.

The eliminatory function tries to localize the discharges to the inner ear. When parents see their child crying in pain from an inflamed ear, they run to the doctor, who then inappropriately interprets this to be an infective process and antibiotics are administered. Antibiotics suppress the symptoms further but do nothing to help resolve the deeper problem of the infectious agent that needs to be eliminated. They also change the intestinal flora, which then impairs digestive function.

Chronic blockage of the ear results in poor verbal and vestibular stimulation and uninhibited primitive reflexes. This delay in inhibition of those reflexes obscures hearing and in turn causes speech delays. Development of higher brain function does not occur, and social and personality development, as they are so intricately connected to all systems, fails to follow its normal course.

Effects of Vaccines in Larger Populations

The model of herd immunity – the concept of vaccinating a percentage of individuals to protect the unvaccinated – is only one possible interpretation of collective responses to infectious disease. This concept is based upon natural disease exposure that promotes life-long, cell-mediated immunity. Vaccination stands as an artificial manipulation of the system.

Vaccine proponents claim it is reasonable to accept the broad range of vaccine adverse effects in the vulnerable population of children as acceptable losses in this perceived greater good.

Now we have an entire system of public education set up to accommodate the needs of those children with pervasive developmental delays.

With this model, there is no allowance for those who have a susceptibility to the adverse effects of vaccination.[28] Furthermore, vaccines are not 100% effective and outbreaks of disease continue to be reported in areas where vaccination compliance is high.[29] This is due, in part, to the natural adaptation and mutation of bacteria and viruses.

Vaccines have been relied upon because until now the homeopathic method of prevention and treatment of infectious disease has not been developed and adopted on a large scale.

Effects of HPx in Larger Populations

On the other hand, the use of HPx in a large enough group of people addresses herd immunity in another way. It stimulates the morphogenetic field of a larger population.[30] This phenomenon is in accordance with the morphogenetic field effect which states that all living organisms operate within a field of relativity. Furthermore, each organ system within the individual exists within its own field. These fields are responsive to, and affected by, energetic and biochemical stimuli.

According to this concept, genes act energetically upon every field of the organism. This in turn impacts the development and function of certain organ systems.

Individuals each possess their own field that may be energetically stimulated, while families, cultures, races, and nationalities share larger fields. If the individual field is stimulated in one instance, the rest of the population is simultaneously affected. In this way, HPx driven cell-mediated immunity, which is energetically affecting not only the energetic field of the individual, but this shared collective field, disease incidence is reduced individually and collectively. This is creating true herd immunity.

Points to Remember:

- More vaccines do not equal more wellness.
- Increased antibody levels may not be synonymous with immunity.
- Vaccine induced artificially generated antibodies last between two and ten years. Naturally acquired antibodies can last a lifetime.
- Additives, adjuvants, and attenuation carry risks.
- Multiple vaccines confuse the immune system.
- Vaccines promote chronic inflammation resulting in deeper pathology.
- The herd immunity is based on naturally acquired disease; vaccination attempts this at the expense of those who can't process vaccines; homeoprophylaxis works at the level of morphogenetic field harming no one.

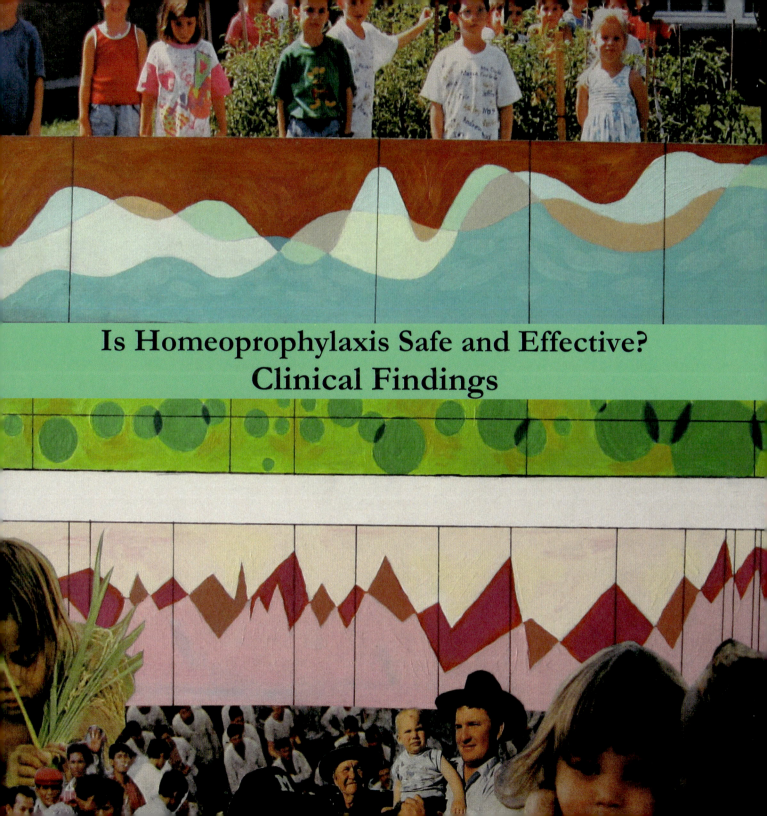

Is Homeoprophylaxis Safe and Effective?
Clinical Findings

Efficacy and Effectiveness

Efficacy is determined by the evidence of antibodies in the blood to specific diseases. This is done by drawing blood to measure titers assessed after disease exposure, vaccination, or homeoprophylaxis.

Efficacy studies are generally not conducted with HPx due to several factors:

- Efficacy studies require a double-blind control group, meaning a completely unprotected group exposed to disease and then tested for antibody levels compared to those receiving HPx.
- This type of study has ethical restraints from putting those who were not protected at risk of developing the disease.
- It is important to note that vaccine efficacy trials are also limited by this ethical consideration and so, rather that exposing children who have either been vaccinated or unvaccinated to an infectious agent, analysis of antibody production is the goal.
- Here the vaccinated group is compared to a control group who receive the vaccine medium without the antigen.
- As we learned in the previous Q and A section on titers, this method of testing antibody production cannot tell us if immunity has developed.

Effectiveness refers to the application of nosodes and remedies in real time disease outbreaks and epidemics with real-world clinicians and clients, with some clients having multiple diagnoses or needs.

The results are noted in terms of actual disease prevalence, not antibody production. The effectiveness of HPx is also determined by patient compliance, disease incidence versus exposure, and general outcomes on health status.

Effectiveness of Homeoprophylaxis

Around the world various effectiveness studies have been conducted utilizing HPx. First discovered by Dr. Samuel Hahnemann, HPx has been responsible for initiating immunity to illnesses such as Meningitis, Japanese encephalitis, Leptospirosis, Polio, Dengue, Covid-19, and other infectious diseases in numerous private and governmentally endorsed interventions.[31]

Effectiveness of a 15-Year Homeoprophylaxis Study in Children in Australia[32]

Dr. Golden has been studying the effectiveness of HPx in 3000 children since 1985. His goal has been to evaluate HPx for disease prevention and to compare HPx with conventional vaccination methods to determine which children would demonstrate better overall health outcomes.

Nosodes used in Golden's research included Pertussin, Pneumococcinum, Haemophilus, Meningococcinum, and Tetanotoxin, and the remedy Lathyrus sativus was used for Polio. All sequentially taken over a period of 84 months.

Previous independent studies revealed that vaccinated children showed an increase in certain conditions including asthma, eczema, ear/hearing conditions, allergies, and behavioral issues. Considering this, Dr. Golden asked participants to complete an annual questionnaire to share data about disease exposure and incidence of these conditions. Participants were also asked what, if any, other vaccinations were used.

A very interesting phenomenon was observed. Those children who had undergone the HPx program without vaccinations were in fact healthier (according to the parameters he studied) than those children who had received constitutional homeopathic care or were vaccinated.

Not only did these children not contract the diseases the nosodes were meant to prevent, but that they had fewer ear, nose, and throat conditions, fewer skin conditions, allergies, asthma, or behavioral conditions than vaccinated children.

This result makes us consider various possible explanations for this outcome. Either these children were impeccably healthy and the HPx program had no impact on their health, or the use of the nosodes not only prevented the respective acute disease but actually removed the tendency to other non-acute disease conditions

From these results, we can conclude that the sequential application of selected nosodes (HPx) both prevents the contraction of disease and stimulates a higher level of health in those who are vaccinated or otherwise left untreated.

Table 1: Comparison of HPx use, with program supplied/not supplied by golden

	All HPx		HPx Only	
	Golden	Not Golden	Golden	Not Golden
Number of Respondents	59	100	25	47
HPx only	42.4%	47.0%		
Vaccination Also	33.9%	31.0%		
General protection Also	44.1%	42.%		
Proportion with Asthma	5.1%	16.0%	0.0%	4.3%
Proportion with Eczema	17.0%	20.0%	4.0%	12.8%
Proportion with Ear/Hearing	15.3%	26.0%	8.0%	21.3%
Proportion with Allergies	23.7%	29.0%	16.0%	12.8%
Proportion with Behavioral issues	8.5%	12.0%	0.0%	6.4%
Proportion with Measles	6.8%	18.0%	0.0%	12.8%
Proportion with Whooping cough	10.2%	17.0%	0.0%	17.0%
Proportion with Mumps	1.7%	1.0%	0.0%	0.0%

Table 1 above, compares the incidence of asthma, eczema, allergies, and behavioral conditions between those who undertook HPx under Golden's supervision (Golden) and other homeopathic practitioners (Not Golden).

It also compares the proportion who contracted measles, whooping cough, or mumps, and compares children who have received some vaccines and those who only used HPx: All HPx refers to those children who received HPx some vaccines, and/or constitutional homeopathy. HPx Only refers to children who only received HPx. Percentages indicate that those children who received HPx Only were healthier across the board.

Table 2 on the next page reveals the results of his fifteen-year study including both partially vaccinated children and those only receiving HPx Only. Here we can see an average of 20% exposure rate to diseases covered by the program. Of which 90% of children exposed did not contract the disease.

The Data Series refers to years of study. E.g., Series 1-5 are participants from the first five years of his study. Responses are the normal immune system action from nosode or remedy stimulation.

Table 2: Summary of results of a fifteen-year study into long-term homeoprophylaxis

Measures of responses & effectiveness after follow-up surveys	Data Series			Totals
	Series 1-5	Series 6-10	Series 11-15	
1. Total responses in previously vaccinated	708	817	817	2342
	73	102	110	285
	10.3%	12.5%	13.5%	12.2%
2. Definite responses to remedies.	50	83	82	215
Responses per person	7.1%	10.2%	10.0%	12.2%
Responses per dose	1.2%	1.7%	1.7%	1.5%
3. Definitely suffered from diseases covered by the main program	18	11	11	40
	2.5%	1.3%	1.4%	1.7%
4. Definitely exposed to diseases covered by main program	177	127	113	417
	25%	15.5%	13.8%	17.8%
5. Definitely suffered from the diseases after taking the remedy	18/177	11/127	11/113	40/417
	10.2%	8.75%	9.7%	9.6%
6. Definitely not suffering diseases after definite exposure and after taking the remedy	159/177	116/127	102/113	377/417
	89.8%	91.3%	90.3%	90.4%

Long-term HPx Study in Children in North America:

Part one: Factors contributing to the successful completion of sequential dosing of disease nosodes.[33]

Method: The purpose of this study is to understand how best to implement and who are candidates for a self-administered 44-month long HPx program. This is a long-term study using real-world participants who may have multiple diagnoses and needs. Part one reviews socio-economic factors that contributed to registration and successful study completion; it involved 682 healthy unvaccinated or partially vaccinated children between the ages of one month and 10 years old. Five percent of the children were over 10 years of age.

Results: Of the 682 children initially registered 50% had no follow-up contact. Of the 37% Completed, 49% Completed in 50 months. 21% Started and Stopped, and 10% Withdrew. The degree of completion of the program was consistent with all ages. Children whose parents had undergraduate degrees, with incomes between $30,000-$50,000 (USD), and never watched TV were more likely to complete the program. Time management issues and lack of understanding were the two main limitations to completion.

Conclusions: When middle class families of unvaccinated and partially vaccinated children understand what they are doing and are supported by competent practitioners they are able to successfully complete this self-administered HPx program.

Part two: Safety of HPx, review of immunological responses, and effects on general health outcomes.[34]

Method: Both unvaccinated and previously vaccinated children registered in a 44-month HPx Program to determine the disease specific immunological effects of HPx and general health outcomes. Individual responses to the respective nosodes/remedies were documented through ongoing and final health status.

Results: Of the 682 registered children, 475 were Unvaccinated and 207 were Previously Vaccinated. Of the total 339 respondents, 226 were Unvaccinated and 113 were Previously Vaccinated (a total of 1,927 previous vaccine-disease doses). A total of 9,333 individual doses were given, which elicited 597 immune responses. Common responses included short-lived fevers, cough, runny nose, restlessness, or sleepiness, change in appetite or stool, and perspiration. Zero adverse events were reported in both cohorts.

General health conditions improved for all who completed the program. Those who completed the program within 50-months, when compared to national averages, experienced above average general health and neurological developmental parameters.

Conclusions: Results demonstrate that HPx offers both unvaccinated and previously vaccinated children a low-risk immunization method that improves general health outcomes. Improved health outcomes in Previously Vaccinated suggests that HPx may be of benefit after previous vaccination.

Effectiveness of Homeopathic Immunization with Meningococcal Disease: Brazil[35,]

In 1974, during an outbreak of meningococcal disease in Brazil, 18,640 children were homeoprophylactically treated to prevent meningococcal infection with one pellet of *Meningococcinum* 30C, and 6,340 were not.

The following results were obtained
- 18,640 protected homeopathically – 4 cases of meningococcal infection.
- 6,340 not protected – 32 cases of meningococcal infection.

Based on the infection (attack) rate in the unprotected group, 94 cases of infection would have been expected in the HPx treated group. Instead, there were only four cases of meningococcal infection, showing that the homeopathic option was 95% effective for preventing meningococcal disease.

These results led to the Brazilian government funding a larger study in 1998, conducted by two professors of medicine from the University Foundation in Blumenau, Brazil and a Blumenau specialist physician and Health City Secretary.

A total of 65,826 people between the ages of 0-20 were treated with one pill of *Meningococcinum* 30C while 23,532 were not.[36]

Over a 12-month period the following results were obtained:
- 65,826 protected homeopathically – 4 cases of meningococcal infection.
- 23,532 not protected – 20 cases of meningococcal infection.

Based on the infection rate in the unprotected group, 58 cases of infection would have been expected in the HPx treated group. Instead, there were only four cases of meningococcal infection. Homeopathic protection offered 95% protection in the first six months and 91% protection over the year for meningococcal disease.

Effectiveness of Belladonna for the Prevention of Japanese Encephalitis: India[37]

A study published in 2010 by researchers at Kolkata's School of Tropical Medicine and the Central Council for Research in Homeopathy showed that the homeopathic medicine Belladonna prevented infection in chick embryos injected with the Japanese Encephalitis virus. The study showed significant decrease in the viral load when treated with the homeopathic medicine *Belladonna* in different potencies, in comparison to placebo, states principal investigator Dr. Bhaswati Bandopadhyay, assistant professor of virology.

Homeoprophylaxis for Dengue: Brazil[38]

In 2008, the State of Rio de Janeiro experienced one of its worst dengue epidemics with more than 250,000 confirmed cases - an increase of 315% compared to 2007, when there were only 67, 000 cases. But in the city of Macaé, just sixty miles north of Rio, the incidence of dengue in the same period fell by 60% due to the use of homeopathic remedies.

The remedies used in formulas or separately were *Eupatorium perfoliatum*, *Phosphorus*, *Crotalus horridus*, *Natrum muriaticum*, and *Arsenicum album* in the 30c dilution. In the first campaign towards Dengue, April-May 2007, 156,000 doses of homeopathic medicine were distributed freely. The entire population of Macaé is estimated at 188,000 inhabitants. In the second season, November-December 2007, some 60,000 doses were distributed. In the third campaign, March 29 to April 25, 2008, 200,000 doses were distributed. In the fourth dosing, 26,000 doses were distributed in November and December 2008. In 2009, 98,708 doses were applied.

The incidence of the disease in the first three months of 2008 fell 93% by comparison to the corresponding period in 2007, whereas in the rest of the State of Rio de Janeiro there was an increase of 128%.

Homeoprophylaxis for Dengue: India[39]

A dengue fever epidemic occurred in Kerala during May-September 2007. More than 100,000 people were affected. After studying the affected cases, the HPx remedy selected by RAECH was *Bryonia alba* 30c. 4 globules, twice daily, for 5 days was administered to 3543 people. 2699 people who took the intervention did not contract Dengue.

Average protective rate of all wards studied was 76.2%.[40]

Homeopathic Immunizations for the Prevention of Leptospirosis: Cuba[41]

Leptospirosis is a serious bacterial disease found primarily in the tropics where the incidence peaks in rainy seasons. Spread by the urine and feces of rats and other vermin, it starts with flu-like symptoms and can progress to nervous system, kidney or liver pathology resulting in death in 5%-40% of cases.

Natural disasters cause a more rapid spread and represent a big challenge to leptospirosis prevention strategies, especially in endemic regions. Vaccination is an effective option but not readily available in emergency situations. Sufficient vaccine doses require one year of production, refrigeration, and needles to apply. Homeoprophylactic interventions can be produced in a short amount of time (two weeks) with no need for refrigeration and can be administered orally. Accordingly, they are ideal for use in emergency epidemics. This is an added advantage in economically challenged countries.

Drs. Gustavo Bracho and Concepcion Campa Huergo of the Findlay Institute conducted the first ever large-scale homeoprophylaxis (HPx) intervention for leptospirosis in three provinces of Cuba in 2007 and 2008. 2.3 million doses were administered each year. The cost of the study was only $200,000 Cuban peso (CP) as compared to the $3 million CP annual vaccination cost for the leptospirosis program already in place. This is stunning economical savings compared to conventional vaccination.

The following table compares the predictive incidence of leptospirosis to those provinces where HPx was applied (IR) and the rest of the country (RC). In 2007 the *Leptospirosis nosode* was introduced in the 200C potency and then repeated in 2008 in the 10M potency. The total annual incidence was reduced by 84% in the (IR) treated region to a total of 2-3 cases in 2008. Incidence rose in the non-intervention region (RC) by 21%, to 150 cases. The research considered other variables that may have influenced the trend but found them to be statistically non-significant.

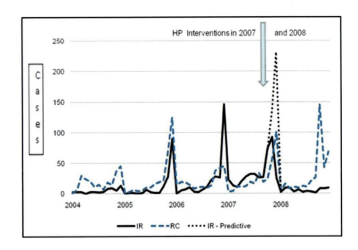

Table 1. Leptospirosis incidence: IR – Intervention Region (Black solid); RC – Rest of the Country (Blue doted), IR-Predictive (Black Dotted).

This table shows that during 2008, based on previous years' incidence rates the Predictive incidence in the Intervention Region in 2007 would have been significantly higher, and in 2008 actual incidence had dropped to nil, versus the Rest of the Country.

Homeoprophylaxis for the Prevention of Polio[42]

For the first half of the nineteenth century polio was rampant in the United States and around the world. In the early 1950's Jonas Salk developed a killed polio vaccine. In 1957 public health care campaigns distributed this vaccine to hundreds of thousands of children. Albert Sabine sought to make the vaccine more effective by creating a live-cell vaccine that would produce long-lasting immunity much like immunity developed from natural disease exposure. In 1962 this polio vaccine was licensed for use. According to public record, these vaccines contributed to the steady decline and gradual eradication of polio in the US and many other countries around the world and their creators have been extolled for their gallant efforts.[43]

Unfortunately, scientists were manipulating data in the 1950's as well. According to vaccine expert Dr. Paul Offit, in his book "The Cutter Incident," "After receiving the Salk vaccine, forty thousand children developed headaches, neck stiffness, muscle weakness, and fever; about two hundred were permanently and severely paralyzed; and ten died…. Children were getting polio even though polio season was still a few months away. And children given the Salk vaccine were actually spreading polio to others (so in fact it was not a killed virus)."

Additionally, evidence has revealed that the HIV virus originated in the early batches of the Sabine polio vaccine shipped to Africa from the monkey kidneys these vaccines were incubated upon.[44] Accordingly, contamination of live-cell vaccines comes with

potentially huge ramifications. Currently there are an estimated thirty-four million people living with HIV/AIDS.[45] It is likely AIDS would not be in existence if it had not been for the development of the Sabine vaccine.

Homeopaths had their own successes with the use of the homeopathic remedy *Lathyrus sativus* for the prevention of Polio. In the 1957 polio epidemic in San Francisco and Chicago, 300 children were given *Lathyrus sativus* and no cases of polio developed, while many children given the Salk vaccine contracted the disease. In the 1957 Buenos Aires epidemic, *Lathyrus sativus* was distributed to 40,000 people and not one case was contracted. Dr. John Bastyr, in 1953, 1956, and 1957, treated polio epidemics and had no polio cases in over 5,000 patients to whom he gave *Lathyrus sativus*.[46] There are no known long-term ramifications for using *Lathyrus sativus* for the prevention of polio.

* Please note that earlier version of this book listed *Lathyrus sativus* polio prevention in the childhood immunological program. Even though historically *Lathyrus sativus* has demonstrated exemplary efficacy towards the prevention of polio FHCi determined that the polio vaccine paradigm propagated fear of polio to their advantage. In our attempts to reduce that fear we have switched out *Lathyrus sativus* and replaced with the *Polio nosode*.

** In time we came to understand that polio virus has been circulating among humans since pre-Egyptian times. The virus was an adaptive mechanism to enable the hunter-gatherer human to become agrarian and digest wheat. Wild polio virus by its own nature down regulates zonulin, which regulates the intestinal tight junctions. Without polio viral strain in the intestines, eating wheat upregulates zonulin.

The wild polio virus, when transmitted from the mother to the child through vaginal childbirth helps to close the tight junctions of the intestinal lining. Wild polio virus when contracted in infancy serves to improve the health of the child's immune and digestive functions.

The polio nosode is now placed as the first nosode in the Full Childhood Immunological HPx Program so as to close the tight junctions of the infants' intestinal lining to improve the digestive and discernment functions of the developing child.[47]

Homeoprophylaxis for Covid-19: India[48]

A total of 22693 individuals of 30 clusters received *Arsenicum album* 30C given twice daily for 7 days. 9493 individuals of 12 clusters were observed in the control group. Results were similar in the medicine and control groups for age, gender, and comorbidity.

The overall protective effect of the *Arsenicum album* 30C was 80.22%: 40 cases per 22693 in the *Arsenicum album* 30C group vs. 84 cases per 9493 in the control group. Adverse effects observed in both groups were mild and resolved without medication and sequelae.

Conclusion: The homeopathic medicine, *Arsenicum album* 30C, was associated with a decrease in the incidence and provided some protection from Covid-19 as compared to non-treatment.

The Safety, Effects, and Efficacy of Covid nosode in Homeopathic Dilution in Humans for Covid-19 Disease Prevention: USA[49, 50]

Homoeoprophylaxis (HPx) with the *Covid nosode*, aims to activate mild, disease specific, short-lived immune responses intended to facilitate the disease process and/or lessen the effects of, or susceptibility to Covid-19 disease expression.

Method: Registration started March 13, 2020, prior to the initial peak of cases in the United State. registrants undertook a self-administered dosing schedule of *Covid nosode* in various potencies. To establish safety, effects, and efficacy of *Covid nosode* registrants of all age groups, from pregnant women and children to the elderly, registered a completed initial health profile, a two-week follow-up, and a three-month follow-up during the initial peak season of Covid-19: March 2020-October 2020.

Results: A total of 1169 people of all age groups registered in the study. Of these 846 responded to follow-up. Peak dosing dates took place prior to the spring surge in cases. A total of 3181 administered doses were reported from 796 respondents during the two-week follow-up period. A total of 2741 symptoms and/or changes in symptoms were reported in all organ systems. Of the 89 respondents with previous disease expression, 17 were unresolved, 16.5 of which recovered after nosode administration. Of the 62 respondents with active disease expression upon registration, there was a 96.77% resolution rate. Of the 135 with known exposure to individuals with previous or active disease, 56 developed random short-lived mild proving symptoms from the nosode of which 98.7% resolved by the end of the dosing period, none developed Covid-19-like disease. Of the total 434 three-month respondents, zero developed Covid-19-like disease indicating that the HPx dosing was 100% effective in preventing disease.

Conclusions: Regardless of age of participant or previous health condition, the *Covid nosode* can be used before, during, or after demonstration of Covid-19 symptom expression, to prevent disease, mitigate active disease and resolve past disease. With no associated adverse events reported, these results suggest *Covid nosode* offers the world a low-risk disease prevention method that is 100% effective in those with definite exposure that deserves consideration in public health programs.

Homeopathic Proving of Coronavirus Nosode[51]

Introduction: The human immunological response to severe acute respiratory syndrome SARS CoV-2 viral infection can range from mild activation and resolution to severe symptoms leading to complete system collapse and death, or prolonged post viral conditions.[52] Homeopathy and homeoprophylaxis (HPx) both offer an opportunity to treat people in an epidemic with the infectious disease agent nosode. This can be applied, according to the Law of Similars, to cure active cases if you have a Materia Medica of the substance to compare to, and in the form of HPx, the disease-specific nosode can prevent disease.[53, 54, 55]

Method: Several doses of *Covid nosode,* 1M potency, were given to 1169 participants. Short-term follow-up captured the immunological and specific organ system symptoms that came and went. These symptoms were collated and evaluated to determine the nosodes' Materia Medica so that it could be applied in active cases according to the 'Law of Similars.'[56]

Results: Over 2500 individual new and cured symptoms in all organ systems related to Covid-19 disease expression, including the mental and emotional effects were cataloged and published in repertory software.

Conclusions: *Covid nosode* not only activated mild short-lived proving symptoms and facilitated the immune process necessary to resolve active cases but transmuted the fear of disease into wellbeing of the participants and contributed to this transformation of the collective as we all moved through the Covid- 19 pandemic.

Points to Remember about HPx:

- 3000 children under HPx protection, over fifteen years, showed great results in Australia.
- Over 9,333 doses of HPx Nosodes were given to children and not a single adverse event was reported in the USA.
- 18,000 protected from meningitis in Brazil.
- Leptospirosis nosode in Cuba protected two million.
- Prophylaxis for dengue reduced incidence by 60% in 2007 and 93.8% in 2008 in Brazil
- Prophylaxis efficacy for dengue in 2007 in India was 72.6%.
- 100% success rate with the use of *Lathyrus sativus* for prevention in polio epidemics in 1953, 1956 and 1957.
- Coronavirus prevention was 100% effective in 135 individuals with definite exposure during the study period with *Covid nosode.*
- Using a nosode in an epidemic contributes not only to the development of immunity of the individual but has the potential to positively affect entire populations.
- Infectious disease and epidemics are not only immunological events but effect the psychological and wellbeing of the individuals involved.
- Nosodes can have a positive effect on the mental and emotional fears regarding infectious disease and the socio-economic-political context within which the disease arises.

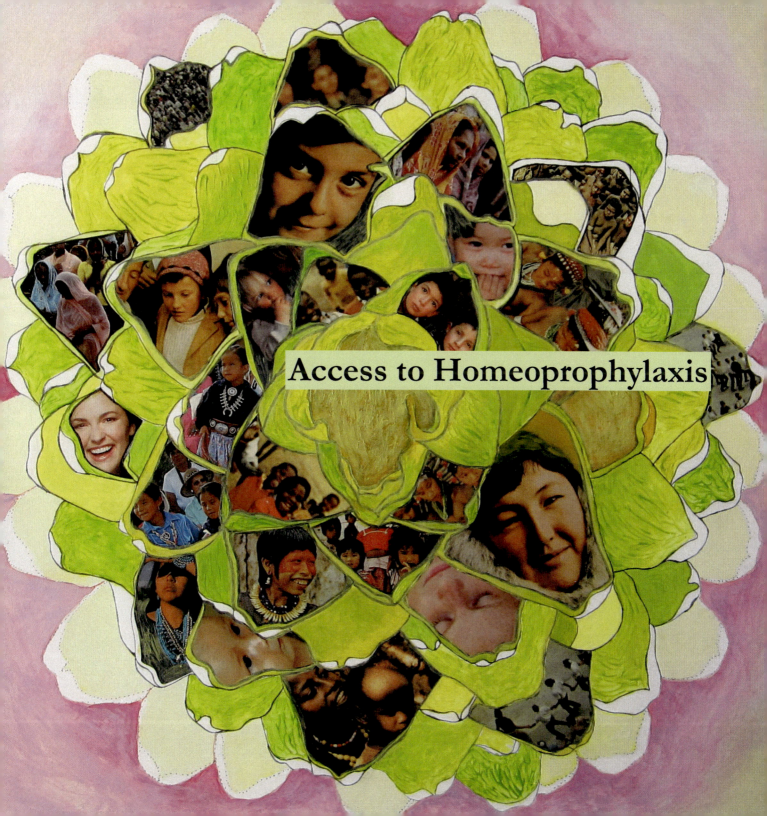

Access to Homeoprophylaxis

Public health models must acknowledge the individuals' sovereignty over their own body

Current Public Healthcare Systems

Currently the world is involved in a huge health experiment. This experiment involves injecting millions of children of every race, culture, and ethnicity with infectious disease agents combined in solutions of various preservatives, contaminants, adjuvants, and genetic material from pathogenic, animal, and human sources in the hopes of preventing infectious disease.

This experiment is driven by the World Health Organization (WHO), the Centers for Disease Control (CDC), The National Institute of Health (NIH), the Food and Drug Agency (FDA) of the United States, vaccine manufacturers around the globe, local and federal governments, wealthy businessmen (Bill Gates Foundation), and many well-meaning others with various political and monetary interests. While these organizations may have initially been established to serve humanity, financial interests and personal corruption have taken them over. No longer are they operating as public servants, they are dictating public health policy to the detriment of individuals' health.

The vaccine industry is one of the largest global economic powers profiting from its global campaign of infectious disease prevention based on an outdated theory of contagion and immune system function.

The global vaccine industry was valued at $24 billion in 2009 and is expected to reach $52 billion in 2016 at a Compounded Annual Growth Rate (CAGR) of 11.5%.[57]

In 2019 (pre-covid) market information for access to vaccines estimates the market value for vaccines to be $33 billion, 2% of the overall pharmaceutical market.[58]

This experiment is driven by fear of disease rather than any understanding of the purpose of disease. It is being performed against the will of the individual, and unwittingly by those who believe that vaccines will save them. This experiment is being done with no risk to the producers and promoters of vaccines or to the doctors vaccinating our children because national laws protect them from any legal or monetary responsibility for any damage that occurs.[59]

The Vaccine Adverse Events Reporting System (VAERS) was established in 1990 and co-managed by the CDC and FDA to serve as a post market survalence system. However, like other voluntary reporting systems, VAERS has several limitations, including unverified reports, underreporting, inconsistant data quality, and absence of a control group that is not vaccinated to give us clear data on the actual numbers of children injueed by vaccines.

This program is an outgrowth of the National Childhood Injury Act, which requires health professionals to report:

- Any event previously listed by the vaccine manufacturer as a contraindication to subsequent doses of the vaccine.
- Any event listed in the Reportable Events Table that occurs within the specified time period after vaccinations which evaluates on a case by case basis.

VAERS is meant to act as a sort of early warning system – a way for the physician and researchers to identify unforeseen reactions or side-effects of vaccination for further study.

The Vaccine Injury Compensation Program went into effect in 1986 to compensate individuals and families of individuals who have been injured by childhood vaccines. However, this program evaluates on a case-by-case basis and compares with the 'documented vaccine safety studies' produced by the CDC. Despite these safety studies being under investigation for fraud, the effect of this comparison results in denial of the vaccine injury and non-compensation of the plaintiff's injuries.

The problem with this experiment is that no one at any level of organization is keeping tabs on the long-term health outcomes of our children.

For those of you who have found this book after the Covid-19 Pandemic and the Covid vaccine, you know we speak the truth. Every one of the international and national organizations and systems in place for disease prevention have colluded to manufacture a pandemic and have rushed to the rescue with a genetically modifying vaccine that has reaped billions of dollars for the stakeholders at the expense of humanity.[60]

Those nations that wanted to choose not to participate in the theatrics of this schema were economically blackmailed into submission to this global agenda. Under the guise of public charity, the largest fraud and assault on individual sovereignty has been played. It will take ten to twenty years of litigation, and whistle blowers to rectify the fallout of such an agenda.

Meanwhile the health of individuals and nations has been deleteriously deranged from the effects of the mRNA vaccine and its gain of function process.

Within, the US there were three types of exemptions to vaccines: religious, medical, and philosophical. In the 12 years since the first edition of this book state by state, exemptions to vaccines have been stripped away and replaced by mandatory vaccine schedules that have no regard for the developing maturity and individual susceptibilities of the recipients to the vaccines.

Moreover, medical professionals who refuse to participate in these vaccination programs are economically and legally sanctioned.

In a democracy is up to you as parents and consumers to lobby your state representatives to ensure your choices in health care will be protected.

Rational Public Healthcare Systems

To create a world where public healthcare campaigns are effective and pose the least risk to the individual, these campaigns can either be locally controlled and disseminated or can call open more centrally organized infrastructure for rapid-small-cell (locally organized and administered) mitigation of disease outbreaks. There is a need to be coherently organized from a central agency to federal and state governments, drug manufacturing facilities, educational institutions, and the local clinics administering the medication.

The core impetus for public healthcare campaigns must arise from the state of benevolence.

The system must be free of political and financial interests and must be socially and monetarily held accountable for its mandates. The research must be ethically and truthfully conducted by organizations that do not have a vested interest in the outcome. The administrators of campaigns carrying potential risk of harm must be held accountable for damages done.

There are few countries in the world that are outside of the reaches of the current corrupt and monetarily driven vaccine market.

Cuba, long held as having one of the best medical systems in the world, is set apart economically and geographically. The leptospirosis study could never have been achieved if Cuba did not operate outside the United States' trade embargo. Cuba has fended for itself. It had remained free from any monetary or political interests of multinational pharmaceutical companies in its efforts to keep its nation strong and healthy.

In 1992 there was an epidemic of a post chickenpox-viral neuralgia that swept the island affecting some 50,000 people. The Cuban government put out an international call for medical assistance. Some homeopaths responded to the situation, determined the appropriate homeopathic remedies, and the epidemic quickly resolved.[61]

As a result of the tremendous success of homeopathy, The Cuban Society of Bioenergetic and Natural Medicine, served as a catalyst to incorporate homeopathy into the National Health System in 1992. Driven by the impetus of the WHO's 2003 mandate that alternative and traditional medicines should be incorporated into a nation's health care system, Cuba has continued to expand the availability of homeopathy in the educational system and through local clinics.

Since then, the Cuban Ministry of Public Health has made great advancements in the development of homeopathy as a diagnostic medical system based on evidence. The Ministry pursues homeopathic investigations with the scientific rigor characteristic of Cuban medicine.

The results of utilizing homeopathy for the treatment and prevention of infectious disease has led to the successful prevention of tuberculosis, hepatitis A, viral conjunctivitis, H1N1 influenza, and leptospirosis.[62] Continued work with Dr. Isaac Golden has served to incorporate an HPx program in various parts of the island. This all changed in the last decade and those in

power of the World Economic Forum (WEF) bated and switched agendas.

Conversely, in the United States and around the world, rather than having systems designed to help people they are set up such with continuing pressures to take away individual rights and exemptions to choose by mandating all vaccines without regard of the short and long-term health status of the recipients.

It is a basic human right to have freedom to choose what we do and do not put in our bodies.

There is minimal public awareness of the availability of HPx, lack of education about HPx in the homeopathic school systems, and legal issues regarding the access of homeopathic nosodes. These challenges must be overcome to freely access homeoprophylaxis in other countries besides Cuba.

It is through small pockets of individuals who want to best serve the health interests of their children and who want to serve society through their part in keeping disease incidence down that HPx has grown.

It is our goal, with this book, to expand the awareness of HPx. In time, we hope to see larger numbers of homeopaths versed in the use of HPx. We hope to see universities and medical institutions intrigued by the work and willing to take it to the next level. We need our public officials to adjust licensing laws to make nosodes more accessible. Eventually we would like to see HPx endorsed by the World Health Organization.

Currently homeopathic nosodes are available from homeopathic pharmacies in the United Kingdom,

Europe, Brazil, Australia, and India. Various practitioners and clinics throughout the world are offering HPx, or are in the process of making HPx programs available.

Expansion of HPx requires that we speak up and continue to expand awareness. Talk to your pediatrician and mention the availability of the HPx option for infectious disease prevention. Point out the fifteen-year study done by Dr. Golden and its excellent results.[63] Certainly, speak to your neighbors, your relatives, and friends about the effectiveness of homeoprophylaxis and why you are choosing this option for your family.

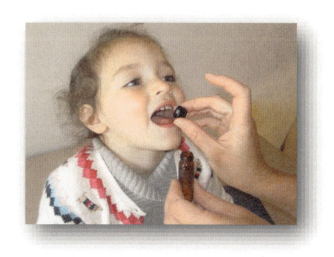

Free and Healthy Children International (FHCi)

FHCi, 501(c)3, was created in 2011 as a central organization to research, provide education about, and develop a mechanism of access to HPx.

FHCi trains and certifies practitioners around the world. These HPx Practitioners are then able to offer homeoprophylaxis supervision to those looking to use HPx for their family. Through epidemiological monitoring FHCi has keep abreast of disease outbreaks and through their internal communication systems HPx Practitioners are able to assist families in participating in HPx Programs with the most up-to-date information regarding the application of selected HPx programs.

Since its inception in 2009, FHCi has completed two large research projects on the use of HPx. Through this research FHCi has confirmed the efficacy of HPx and more importantly its assertions and understanding about health, infectious disease, and the use of nosodes has exponentially increased.

The first research, published in 2019 and 2020, was a duplicate and confirmation of the long-term research on childhood immunization conducted by Dr. Isaac Golden.[64,65] Accordingly, this first research poised FHCi in February of 2020 to conduct research with a large-scale HPx application for Covid-19 prevention.[66]

FHCi will continue to provide an avenue to access and research for All New HPx Programs.

Private Member Associations

Given the limitations of the existing legal and medical climate regarding the right of the people to access the medical procedures of their choice, the threats against practitioners practicing outside of the legally recognized norm, and the threats of annihilation of the homeopathic and natural medicine industry through legislative censorship, there is the necessity to realize our God-given-rights to private assembly and access to the health care options of our choice under common law. These rights must be protected, not only for people choosing homeopathy for themselves, or for practitioners practicing homeopathy, but also for the producers of nosodes, remedies, and medicaments we need.

Moreover, FHCi acknowledges the God-given-right of the people to privacy and the right to accept or refuse any medical treatment.

Accordingly, FHCi has identified an independent Private Member Association to provide unfettered access to HPx to its members. This association has been established to form member-to-member relationships between the HPx Practitioner and those undertaking HPx, and to gather and house data substantiating the use of HPx.

For access to a practitioner trained in homeoprophylaxis please refer to freeandhealthychildren.org to become a patron. Upon registration, patrons will be referred to the associated Private Member Association's Practitioner Directory to continue their journey in immune system education using nosodes

100

Points to Remember:

- The role of the immune system is to govern our body.
- The role of government is to protect people from harm.
- Individual or corporate financial interests should not pressure governments to mandate or censure any health care measure.
- In the United States, in some states, individuals have medical, religious, and philosophical exemptions to mandatory vaccines.
- It is our God given right to assemble privately, and to maintain sovereignty over our and our children's bodies.
- Individuals with healthy immune systems will exert their autonomy and sovereignty.
- To secure the right to health, an individual must be able to exercise his/her fundamental right to privacy and self-determination and the right to make personal choices in pursuit of health, healing, well-being, and survival.[67]
- Individuals who voluntarily choose HPx for disease prevention and immune education are contributing towards a reduction in infectious contagious disease incidence and the betterment of their health and that of society.

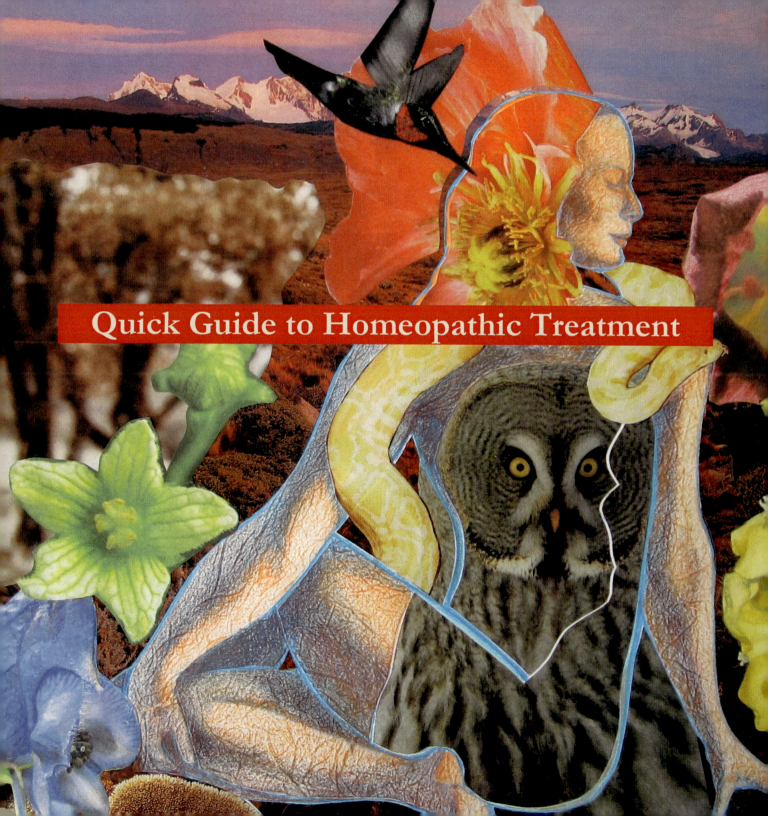

Quick Guide to Homeopathic Treatment

Overview of Homeopathic Prescribing

The following section gives a brief description of the diseases in the current United States vaccine schedule, seasonal and epidemic disease, and tropical diseases. Each disease entry overviews the symptomology and potential hazards and lists a few homeopathic remedies that can be used for treatment.

This guide does not provide an exhaustive list of remedies, the indications for a particular remedy, nor does it address all complications that can arise. The main takeaway from this guide is that every infectious disease can be treated effectively with homeopathy, under the care of a practitioner.

While most of the diseases listed in this guide are generally self-limiting and relatively easy to treat with homeopathy, depending on the health of the individual in relationship to a particular disease, some serious complications can occur.

When in doubt consult your local practitioner or go to your nearest hospital.

While it is possible to become proficient in homecare with homeopathy, this guide does not replace the consultation of a trained homeopathic practitioner nor the need for further education in homeopathy. This is merely for reference to demonstrate that there are homeopathic remedies specific to infectious diseases. Reference to therapeutic manuals will assist one in working with homeopathy.

According to the "Law of Similars" remedies are selected based on similarity between the symptoms a remedy can produce in a healthy person and the symptoms of the sick person.[68]

In most situations, the correct remedy will hasten the process of the disease and will ensure that the process of disease continues to resolution while reducing the damaging effects of the disease.

With the correct remedy, you may see an initial increase in fever but can expect a rapid change of state, from pain and agitation to calm, which will be the first step towards recovery. Often one remedy is all that is needed to complete the circle of disease process. In some situations, different remedies may be needed at the beginning, middle and end point of this cycle.

Insufficient fever can also be an issue; bluish or purple discoloration of skin, listlessness, and bad breath as signs that the fever is turning septic. **Seek Professional Help at this time.**

It is the symptom presentation of the persons' response during the illness that is used to guide one's prescription, not the diagnosis. Accordingly, different people may respond differently to the same disease entity. In these cases, a different remedy would be needed for each person with the same disease. Conversely, as different diseases stimulate similar symptom presentations, the same remedy may be used for different diagnoses.

Most homeopathic remedies are available over the counter at local health food stores and can be given according to the directions listed on the bottle. Over the counter remedies are available in the 30C potency.

- A dose consists of three pellets.
- Most conditions will respond curatively to two or three doses of the selected remedy given over a few hours.
- Doses may need to be repeated over the following days to ensure complete recovery.
- As symptom pictures change towards recovery adjunctive remedies may be needed.
- Observing and reporting the most limiting and pronounced symptoms to your practitioner will assist them in choosing the best remedy.

Even if one does not know the exact diagnosis of the acute disease it is still possible to accurately, and effectively treat with homeopathy because remedies are selected based on similar symptom presentation not on diagnosis alone.

Chickenpox

Chickenpox, the symptoms expression of active Varicella-zoster virus, is a common, highly infectious, acute viral disease with mild constitutional symptoms and vesicular skin eruptions. The disease is spread by contact with blisters, or aerosol droplets through sneezing, coughing, or saliva exchange from an infected person. The incubation period is two to three weeks, and the person remains infectious until all the scabs have healed up. Pneumonia may develop in some cases.

Signs and Symptoms

- Slight fever, runny nose, headache, backache, loss of appetite, and general weakness.
- Within a day or two, red spots appear: usually on the back and chest first.
- The spots enlarge and develop into vesicles with a red base that become filled with a clear liquid.
- The eruptions can be very itchy.
- After a day or two, the fluid turns yellow, and a crust or scab develops which eventually dries and falls off.

Main Remedies

- *Antimonium crudum*
- *Mercurius*
- *Rhus toxicodendron*
- *Stramonium*

Seek Professional Help When

- Eruptions fail to appear.
- Chest becomes full of mucous.
- Eruptions are getting infected or failing to scab over.

Rhus toxicodendron – Poison ivy

Measles

Measles is a relatively mild, highly contagious, eruptive disease related to the Morbillivirus which is spread by droplet infection. The incubation period is nine to fourteen days. It takes two to four days for the rash to develop, which then subsides after two or three more days.

Signs and symptoms

- The first symptoms are watery eyes, runny nose, and fever.
- The fever rises after which small white dots appear on the gums and insides of the cheeks.
- During the fever, a rash appears at the hairline, which spreads downward eventually covering the body, and coalescing into larger patches.
- The fever subsides and the rash dries and forms a fine scaling and flaking appearance.
- Rash resolves in a few days.

German Measles(Rubella)

German measles, is the expression of active Rubella virus, presents with vary similar but less severe symptoms than measles. It is spread by droplet infection. Its incubation period is about sixteen days after which a fine rash develops and passes on its own after the fourth day. The concern with German measles is its effect on unborn fetuses in pregnant women in which it can cause growth retardation, deafness, and other congenital problems.

Signs and symptoms

- Non-specific cold like symptoms followed by enlarged cervical glands causing pain on moving the neck.
- Mild fever develops.
- A fine bumpy rash starts on the face and spreads down the body.
- Rash resolves in a few days.

Main Remedies for Measles and German Measles

- *Belladonna*
- *Euphrasia*
- *Gelsemium*
- *Pulsatilla*
- *Apis*
- *Stramonium*
- *Zinc*

Seek Professional Help When

- Rash fails to appear.
- Child makes high pitched cries and moans.
- Fever goes over 103°F or is insufficient to bring out rash.
- Rash fails to resolve.

Pulsatilla nigrans –Pasque flower

Haemophilus Influenzae

Haemophilus influenzae type b is a bacterium that is believed to be responsible for a variety of invasive syndromes particularly severe in infants. It is a bacterium that normally resides in the mucous membranes but can become a risk in infants and young children. Breast feeding and passive immunity from the mother protect the infant in the early months. It is not known how these normal bacteria become pathogenic and develop into invasive diseases.

Signs and Symptoms

- The meningitis symptoms are listed in the following section.
- Epiglottitis begins with swelling between the base of the tongue and epiglottis with a very high fever. The swelling of the epiglottis results in a dry croaking voice, difficulty inspiring or expiring, and blockage of the airways resulting in suffocation.
- Cellulitis is a rapidly progressing potentially life-threatening skin infection that usually involves the face, head, or neck.

Meningitis

Meningitis is inflammation of the cerebral and spinal meninges: the membrane that covers the brain and spinal cord. This inflammation can be a result of either viral illness or meningococcal bacterial strains, or systemic reaction to another illness such as Haemophilus bacteria. The condition is classified as a medical emergency due to the proximity of the brain and possibility for brain damage. If meningitis is suspected, give the indicated remedies on the way to the hospital.

Signs and Symptoms

- Headache, neck stiffness, arching of the back, with a high fever, confusion, or altered consciousness, and possibly seizures.
- Inability to tolerate light or loud noises.
- Nausea, vomiting and tiredness.
- If the condition is bacterial there may be a fine blotching of the skin (small areas of broken blood vessels).
- The condition may become septic, with rapid heart rate and breathing.

Main Remedies for Haemophilus and Meningitis

- *Aconite*
- *Apis*
- *Belladonna*
- *Bryonia alba*

Seek Professional Help When

- Child makes high pitches cries and moans.
- Child has a stiff neck or is arching their back.
- There is insufficient fever, and the child is suffering
- Fever goes over 103°F.
- Throat and airways become constricted.
- Skin lesions are becoming infected.

Belladonna – Deadly nightshade

Influenza

Influenza is an acute viral infection of the respiratory system. Viral strains of influenza change from year to year and are related to avian flu species. The virus is spread by coughing and sneezing and by coming into contact with objects contaminated by mucus from an infected person.

The virus enters the body though the respiratory tract. Incubation period is one to three days. The person is most contagious one day before the onset of symptoms and for up to seven days after the symptoms begin. Fatigue and resultant cough can last for several weeks.

Signs and Symptoms

- Sudden onset of fever and chills, headaches, malaise, muscle aches, and pains.
- Sore throat, nasal congestion, and cough.
- There can also be gastrointestinal disturbances and neuralgia.
- Complications include secondary infections of the ear, sinuses, and lungs.

Main Remedies

- *Bryonia alba*
- *Eupatorium perfoliatum*
- *Ferrum phosphoricum*
- *Gelsemium*
- *Rhus toxicodendron*

Seek Professional Help When

- Fever renders the child listless.
- Lungs fill with fluid.
- Pain in lungs on breathing or coughing.
- Fever lasts more than 2-3 days.
- If it looks like pneumonia is developing.

Eupatorium perfoliatum –Boneset

Covid-19

The Rhinovirus SARS CoV-2 is believed to be the cause of Covid-19 disease expression. There are two aspects to this virus. One is the infectious agent of the modified SARS virus, and the other is the spike protein attached to the virus, which attaches to angiotensin receptors (ACE2 receptors) throughout the body. The angiotensin system regulates blood pressure, fluid balance, and governs constriction/relaxation in the lungs and intestines.

Symptom expression can occur within 1-2 days of exposure. If left untreated can last 3-4 days, or as long as several weeks. Long-haul Covid-19 occurs if the immune system is previously suppressed or laden with other retroviruses that become activated through infection

Those individuals with a higher number of ACE2 receptors and other comorbidities such as diabetes, high blood pressure, obesity, or are smokers are at increased risk of more severe disease expression and death.

The human immunological response to acute respiratory syndrome Covid-19 disease expression can range from mild symptoms leading to resolution, to severe symptoms leading to complete system collapse, death, or prolonged post disease conditions.

Signs and Symptoms

- Fear and terror relating to getting sick.
- Fever, chills, body aches, sinus issues, scratchy throat, and other general symptoms.
- Dry or constrictive cough, difficulty breathing, or hypoxia.
- Vomiting and/or diarrhea.

- In some cases, increased bleeding or circulatory issues prevail.

Main remedies

- *Arsenicum album*
- *Bryonia alba*
- *Rhus toxicodendron*
- *Carbo vegetabilis*

Seek Professional Help When

- There is prolonged respiratory distress.
- Oxygen levels fall below 92%.
- There is prolonged vomiting or diarrhea.

Professional treatment is required

Carbo vegetabilis– Charcoal

Mumps

Mumps is the expression of active Mumps virus which is in the same family of viruses as influenza. Mumps is a relatively mild disease, producing inflammation in one or both parotid glands. It is passed from person to person via droplet infection. The incubation period is eighteen days and the sickness usually lasts three to ten days. The inflammation may metastasize to the breast or gonads and cause infertility if not properly treated.

Signs and Symptoms

- Moderate to high fever, headache, and fatigue.
- Within 24 hours there is earache and swelling of one or both parotid glands giving the face an extremely swollen look.
- Pain and tenderness on swallowing. Sour foods and drinks increase the pain as it causes the glands to salivate.

Main Remedies

- *Jaborandi*
- *Phytolacca*
- *Pulsatilla*
- *Trifolium repens*

Seek Professional Help When

- In 10 to 14-year-old children the risk of sterility increases.
- Glands suddenly stop being swollen is a sign of metastasis.

Trifolium repens – White clover

Pneumonia

Pneumonia is classified as an infectious disease process, but not as a contagious disease. Streptococcus pneumoniae, which normally resides in the lungs is held responsible for 90% of all bacterial pneumonia. Pneumonia may also have a viral basis or result from aspiration of food or other particles. Pneumonia may be the primary disease but more often is a complication of other diseases.

Pneumonia sets in when resistance is lowered by severe colds, influenza, whooping cough, chickenpox, general poor health, or loss of vital heat. When excess fluid accumulates in the lungs it provides a fertile ground for pneumonia to develop. The resultant inflammation of the lungs and consolidation of tissue can become life threatening. Insufficient fevers can lead to pneumonia settling in. Death can occur by suffocation.

Signs and Symptoms

- High fever with chills, weakness, with pain or burning in the chest.
- Weak cough with oppressed breathing, rapid or shallow breathing with rapid pulse.
- Blood streaked or brown fluid is coughed up.

Main Remedies

- *Apis*
- *Bryonia alba*
- *Ferrum metallicum*
- *Phosphorus*

Seek Professional Help When

- There is pain on breathing or coughing.
- Child is using upper chest and neck muscles to breathe.
- The chest sounds full of fluid.

Bryonia alba – White bryony

Tetanus

Tetanus, or lockjaw, is a neurological condition caused by a neurotoxin released by the bacteria *Clostridium tetani* in a contaminated wound. This bacterium is found in rural areas, specifically in soil and dust, and spread by animal and human feces. It is also normally present on your skin especially if you walk barefoot and or live in farmland. It only becomes pathological if it enters puncture wounds of the body.

Free bleeding and washing the wound thoroughly minimizes the likelihood of tetanus infection. The incubation period of tetanus averages eight days after the time of infection.

Signs and Symptoms

- Fine red lines radiating out from the wound demonstrating the infection and inflammation of the surrounding nerves.
- Radiating pain and/or twitching in the muscles as the neurotoxin travels up the nerve.
- Within 48 hours, the person can experience difficulty opening the mouth, hence the name "lockjaw."

- Progressing muscle spasms causing rigidity of the back and grimacing of the face.
- Light, noise, and movement can trigger muscle spasms, or they can be nearly constant.

Main Remedies

- *Hypericum*
- *Ledum*

Seek Professional Help When

- Wounds are not thoroughly cleaned.
- Puncture wounds do not bleed freely.
- Red lines emanate from wound.
- There are twitching muscles around the wound.

Ledum palustre – Wild rosemary

Whooping Cough

Whooping cough, also known as pertussis, is the result of a respiratory tract infection with the bacteria Bordetella pertussis. The bacteria are spread through coughing and sneezing. The incubation period is usually about seven days and active disease may last up to one-hundred days without treatment.

The cough which becomes violent and spasmodic after the acute phase may continue for weeks or months. It is a relatively mild disease except in infants who may choke on the mucus during the catarrhal phase or suffocate from the cough during the spasmodic phase.

Signs and Symptoms

- Mild fever in the acute phase with clear mucus in the upper respiratory tract.
- Inflammation of the mucus membranes accompanied by excessive mucus excreted from the throat and upper respiratory tract.
- Prolonged phase of paroxysms of cough ending in prolonged crowing or whooping respiration.
- Complete resolution may take one to two months.

Main Remedies

- *Coccus cacti*
- *Corallium rubrum*
- *Drosera*

Seek Professional Help When

- In infants with known exposure to whooping cough.
- Inspiration becomes very difficult.
- Fits of coughing become violent, and the face turns purple or blue during the cough.

Corallium rubrum – Red coral

Polio

Polio, is an acute contagious entero-viral disease in response to the Poliovirus. This virus is transmitted through water droplets or the fecal-oral route. This virus also regulates the tight junctions of the intestinal tract. If exposed through the natural vaginal childbirth process and if the child is breast fed (mother's milk antibodies) they will be protected for life and the tight junctions of the infant will prepare the infant for the digestion of wheat.

If exposed later in life, and ones consumes a high hybridized wheat diet this virus can slip through the tight junctions and attack the central nervous system, injuring or destroying the nerve cells that control the muscles sometimes causing a temporary paralysis or atrophy of the muscles. Polio is a serious disease but is usually not fatal. The incubation period is one to three weeks. Most cases resolve in ten days without treatment. 5% of the cases result in permanent paralysis.

Signs and Symptoms

- Like influenza: fever, chills, and body-ache.
- High fever, headache, vomiting, sore throat, pain, and stiffness in neck and back, and drowsiness.
- Paralysis most often affects the legs but can involve any muscles including the throat, affecting swallowing; the bladder and bowels affecting elimination; and the diaphragm, affecting breathing.
- The most serious cases cause paralysis of the diaphragm, which can result in death even if mechanical ventilation is used.

116

- In some cases, permanent atrophy of muscles will remain.

Main Remedies

- *Gelsemium*
- *Lathyrus sativus*

Seek Professional Help When

- Influenza-like symptoms relapse after apparent recovery.
- There is excessive stiffness in neck with fever.
- The fever has subsided and then returns with loss of voluntary motion of the limbs.

Gelsemium sempervirens – Yellow jasmine

Rotavirus

Rotavirus is the most common reason for diarrhea among infants and young children. The virus is found in the intestines and transmitted through the fecal-oral route, and it infects and damages the intestinal cells and lining. Once infected it takes about two days before symptoms appear.

Nearly everyone has been infected with the virus at least once and over time immunity is developed. Many people are symptom free carriers.

Risks come with loss of electrolytes and dehydration. Special care must be used to ensure re-hydration with water, sugar, salt, and electrolytes.

Signs and Symptoms

- Symptoms start with vomiting followed by four to eight days of mild to severe diarrhea.
- Diarrhea may be accompanied by a low-grade fever.
- The virus affects the cells of the intestines and may make the child milk intolerant for several weeks after infection.

Main Remedies

- *Arsenicum album*
- *Phosphorus*
- *Podophyllum*
- *Veratrum album*

Seek Professional Help When

- There is excessive loss of vital fluids.
- Fever lasts more than two days.
- The child is not drinking water.

Arsenicum album – White arsenic

Diphtheria

Diphtheria is an acute, highly contagious disease of the nose, throat, and tracheal regions related to the bacteria Corynebacterium diphtheriae. It spreads through mucus and droplets of moisture from the mouth, nose, and throat. The incubation period is two to five days. The onset is rapid and can be severe without proper treatment.

Signs and Symptoms

- Sore throat is accompanied by a headache, fever, and malaise.
- The breath has a sickening smell and the lymph glands in the neck become swollen and tender.
- The membranes lining the nose, throat, and mouth become gray in color.
- The membranes of the affected areas slough off in large sheets and can cause severe blockage of the upper breathing passages.
- The bacterium releases its toxin throughout the body, resulting in life-threatening complications damaging the heart, nerves, and blood, resulting in low platelet count.

Main Remedies

- *Apis*
- *Lac caninum*
- *Mercurius*

Seek Professional Help When

- The fever is over 102°F.
- Child is having difficulty breathing or swallowing.
- Condition is becoming septic.

Apis mellifica – Honeybee

Hepatitis A

Hepatitis A is the expression of the Hepatitis A virus. This disease can present in epidemics or in individual cases. It is spread by the oral-fecal route from contaminated water or food, especially seafood. It is a self-limiting acute disease with complete recovery 95% of the time. In some cases, it causes severe inflammation of the liver which can result in rapid death.

The incubation period is fourteen to fifty days and may last from two to three weeks. The disease is most infectious before the start of the jaundice and up to one week after the jaundice has begun.

Hepatitis B

This is a more serious state of disease and has longer lasting consequences than Hepatitis A.

Hepatitis B is considered to be a sexually transmitted viral disease. It can be transmitted via blood transfusions, bodily fluids such as tears, saliva, and semen. The Hepatitis B virus can persist in bodily fluids for years or even a lifetime if left untreated.

Signs and Symptoms

- Onset of symptoms includes fever, loss of appetite, vomiting, headache, abdominal pain, occasionally diarrhea, general weakness, and uneasiness.
- Yellowing of the eyes.
- After five to ten days the stools become harder and clay colored, the urine is dark and foamy.
- Yellowing of the skin and a raise in temperature with a slow pulse.
- If the condition worsens, the liver and spleen become enlarged, and an intense itching develops.
- An increase in temperature, chill, headache, and nosebleeds or other hemorrhages.
- Urine is scanty with red deposits.
- In Hepatitis B, symptoms appear in the same order as with Hepatitis A but are less intense and will appear over a longer period. The person can eventually die of liver failure.

Main Remedies

While the same remedies may be used to treat both Hepatitis A and B, potency and repetition are different. As Hepatitis A is an acute self-limiting disease, usually a single dose or several doses given over a short period of time will resolve the condition. Hepatitis B has more long term and chronic effects, therefore the remedy may need to be repeated often over a longer period to slow the condition and reverse some of the symptoms.

- *Bryonia alba*
- *Chamomilla*
- *Chelidonium*
- *Phosphorus*

Seek Professional Help When

- All cases of liver insufficiency.
- When skin or eyes have a yellow tinge.
- The stools are white.
- There is red sand in the urine.
- Excessive thirst and loss of appetite.

Chelidonium majus – Greater celandine

Human Papillomavirus

There are over 1200 types of Human papillomavirus (HPV). Of these 18 types are associated with genital warts and increase the potential to develop cancer. Genital warts are produced by the HPV types 1, 2, 6, 11, 16 and 18. HPV is the most common sexually transmitted disease (STD). It is estimated that 1% of sexually active people between the ages of 18 and 45 develop genital warts; however, as many as 40% of sexually active adults carry HPV. Of these adults 5-10% may develop cancer.

About two-thirds of the people who have sexual contact with someone with genital warts develop genital warts. For most people, the body's defense system will clear the virus without treatment. The incubation period is one to six months. Repeated infections and unresolved cases can increase the risk of cervical cancer. The tendency for HPV to activate cervical cancer is a constitutional issue.

Signs and Symptoms

- Warts may be either flat, or resemble raspberries, or cauliflowers in appearance.
- The warts begin as small red or pink growths, often occurring in clusters, and can grow as large as four inches across.
- Warts maybe accompanied by increased vaginal discharge, flu-like symptoms such as backache, headache, swollen glands, fever, or difficulty swallowing.

Main Remedies

- *Nitric acid*
- *Thuja*

Seek Professional Help When

- Discharge persists.
- Warts do not clear on their own after a few weeks.
- There is a family history of cancer.

Thuja occidentalis– White cedar

Sexually Transmitted Diseases

While a number of sexually transmitted disease nosodes are listed and included in several of the HPx Programs described in the **Homeoprophylaxis: The vaccine Alternative** chapter, home prescribing is not recommended for their treatment, including that for HPV, due to the breadth of homeopathic understanding needing in their care.

Sexually transmitted diseases have been active within the human population for thousands of years. They are designed to influence sexual behavior towards the sanctity of sexual intimacy.

Each sexually transmitted disease has primary acute disease symptom presentation and carries secondary and tertiary chronic effects. These tendencies and conditions can carry on to the offspring of those infected. The degree to which these secondary or tertiary chronic aspects are active is relative to the underlying health of the individual. Constitutional homeopathic care is needed to mitigate all aspects of these inherited disease conditions (miasmatic health) Homeoprophylaxis dosing can help to clear these miasmatic conditions in addition to immune system education towards these infectious diseases.

Free and Healthy Children International has developed the **Healthy Sexuality and Pre-Procreation HPx** and **Healthy Pregnancy and Fetal Development HPx Program**, which both include some of the sexually transmitted disease nosodes to not only prevent the diseases but also to mitigate the potential afflictions that arise from any generational imprint.

The concepts, remedies needed, and follow-up care for the treatment of active, and the secondary and tertiary expressions of sexually transmitted disease is beyond the scope of this book.

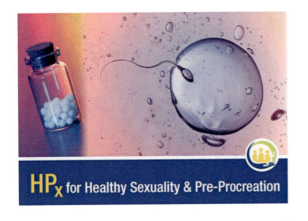

HP$_X$ for Healthy Sexuality & Pre-Procreation

HP$_X$ for Healthy Fetal Development

Tropical Diseases

Homeopathy has a rich history in treating and preventing tropical diseases. There are many existing homeopathic clinics in Africa, Central America, and Asia providing prevention and treatment for diseases such as Malaria, Dengue fever, Yellow fever, Typhoid, and Cholera.

While we have made the argument that the infectious process may serve as a beneficial process for the individual, most tropical diseases can have long-term ramifications or may prove to be fatal. Prevention is advisable.

Incidence of disease is based on the relative strength of the individual, collective susceptibility towards that pathogen and seasonal influences. Accordingly, treating the collective with the appropriate homeopathic remedy will help balance that susceptibility and lower the disease incidence in the entire population.

As many tropical diseases share similar symptomatology, the same remedies may be used for one or more of the diseases discussed. Each disease section lists a few of the main remedies for that disease. Please refer to the other tropical disease pages for other possibilities to match symptom pictures.

As this book serves as a guide and not all remedies are listed, consultation with a practitioner is necessary.

Preventative Measures

Avoid contaminated water and food

- Drink bottled water and food prepared by you or your host family, and in well attended restaurants.
- Avoid ice in your drinks.
- Water purification devices may be necessary.
- Wash all fruits and veggies that do not have peels in purified water and soap.
- Avoid raw foods, salad, etc.
- Avoid some street vendors as the cooking oil may be contaminated.
- Wash your hands often.

Protect yourself from mosquitoes

- Wear long sleeves and pants.
- Sleep under mosquito netting.
- Use mosquito repellent.
- Stay inside during the early morning and evening hours when mosquitoes come out.

Other considerations

- Condition your digestive tract with Probiotics, Colostrum, and Digestive Enzymes for one month before and during travel.
- Have Activated Charcoal on hand to take if digestive upset seems imminent.
- Follow BRAT diet to replace nutrients (Bananas, Rice, Apple sauce, Toast), in cases of diarrhea or electrolyte loss.
- Boiled rice water, Pedialyte, or GatorAid to replace the loss of vital fluids from diarrhea or blood loss.

Cholera

Cholera is an acute diarrheal illness caused by infection of the intestine with the bacterium Vibrio cholerae, and its toxins. Cholera spreads rapidly in areas with inadequate treatment and separation of sewage and drinking water. Diagnosis is confirmed by stool sample.

Incubation time for cholera is twelve hours to six days. Death often occurs due to rapid loss of body fluids leading to dehydration and shock. Without treatment death can occur within hours.

Signs and Symptoms

- Sudden effortless and continuous large quantities of foul-smelling, mucousy diarrhea followed by profuse vomiting.
- Chill and collapse accompanied by violent cramping.
- The febrile stage develops if the patient has survived the first two stages.
- In the most severe cases, there is no improvement but a rapid deterioration ending in death, mostly from kidney failure.

Main Remedies

- *Camphora*
- *Cuprum*
- *Veratrum album*

Seek Professional Help When

- Any infectious process with extreme loss of vital fluids.
- Any infectious process with bruising, or vomiting of black emesis, or black stools.
- Any infectious process with yellowing of the skin.

Professional treatment is required

Veratrum album – White hellebore

Typhoid

Typhoid fever, is a potentially life-threatening disease caused by the bacteria Salmonella typhi. The bacteria are found in contaminated food and water and pass from person to person via the fecal-oral route. Diagnosis is determined by stool sample.

The incubation period is eight to twenty-eight days, and the disease develops in a step-by-step fashion over the next three weeks. Death is a result of dehydration, loss of fluids, and septicemia.

Baptisia – Blue wild indigo

Signs and Symptoms

- Prolonged high fever with chills, abdominal pain, loss of appetite, headache, and prostration.
- Abdominal pain; diffuse or localized in the right lower quadrant of the abdomen accompanied by watery and undigested green stools.
- A spot rash with small red hemorrhagic spots develops on the trunk of the body.
- As the disease progresses in severity, the person becomes more delirious, and experiences altered states of consciousness or even coma.
- Relapse of symptoms is common.
- Death occurs due to bleeding in the intestines causing perforation in the intestinal wall resulting in peritonitis.

Main Remedies

- *Baptisia*
- *Phosphoric acid*
- *Pyrogenium*
- *Rhus toxicodendron*

Professional treatment is required

Dengue Fever

Dengue (DF) and dengue hemorrhagic fever (DHF) are caused by four viral serotypes that are in the genus flavivirus (all related to yellow fever). The dengue virus is transferred to humans by the day-biting mosquito Aedes aegypti.

DF and DHF have an incubation period of three to fourteen days. Infection with one of the dengue fever serotypes provide life-long immunity to only that serotype. Chances of fatality with DF are very low. DHF often occurs in cases of individuals with previous DF infection. Fatalities are more common with DHF.

Signs and Symptoms

DF
- Sudden onset of chills and high fever, severe frontal headache, severe muscle, and backbone pain lasting three to five days.
- Weakness, tastelessness, dry tongue, constipation, reddish eyes, and facial swelling.
- The rash appears three to five days after onset of fever spreading from the torso to the arms, legs, and face.

DHF
- High fever of acute onset.
- Liver enlargement and tenderness, nausea and vomiting, abdominal pain, severe pain in the backbone and joints, and hemorrhage.
- Bleeding under the skin, nosebleeds, bleeding gums, blood in the vomit, and blood in the stool.

Yellow Fever

Yellow fever is an illness caused by a virus in the flavivirus family (tic borne meningitis, dengue fever, West Nile; those diseases that spread through arthropod vectors and is related to the Hepatitis C virus). It is transmitted from person to person in urban areas or monkeys to humans via infected mosquitoes in the jungle.

The incubation period is three to six days. Most cases are very mild, having only a fever and headache, and resolving within forty-eight hours. Other cases will develop more serious complications resulting in internal hemorrhage, organ failure, and ultimate death.

Signs and Symptoms

- Sudden onset fever, headache, and rapid pulse.
- The second day the pulse becomes very slow despite the continued fever.
- Muscle aches, back pain, irritability, insomnia, and a flushed face accompany the fever.
- The illness affects the liver, where the blood clotting mechanism becomes disturbed, resulting in yellowing of the skin and spontaneous bleeding.
- By the third day, nausea begins, accompanied by vomiting of coffee ground-like vomit and excess protein in the urine.
- The fourth day brings a welcomed remission of symptoms for several hours up to two days, only to be followed by an increased systemic toxicity and rapid worsening of the disease resulting in kidney and heart failure.

- Eventually, the person develops an unusual episode of hiccough, which is followed by coma and death within seven to ten days.

Main Remedies for Dengue and Yellow Fever

- *Bryonia alba*
- *Crotalus horridus*
- *Eupatorium perfoliatum*
- *Phosphorus*

Professional treatment is required

Crotalus horridus – American rattlesnake

Malaria

Malaria is a parasitical disease caused by four different plasmodium species: P. falciparum, P. vivax, P. ovale and P. malariae. Malaria is transmitted from human to human via the Anopheles mosquito. The Anopheles bite in the night with most activity at dawn and dusk.

The parasites enter the human host's bloodstream after a bite by an infected mosquito. Once inside the host they migrate to the liver where they multiply. The incubation period varies from seven to thirty days depending on the plasmodium and causes a fever each time the plasmodia are released from the liver. Without proper treatment malaria can become chronic with intermittent fevers affecting the person for life.

Signs and Symptoms

- A classic malaria attack lasts six to ten hours. It starts with a cold stage marked by shivering, a hot stage with fever, headaches, and vomiting, and finally a sweating stage after which the body temp returns to normal with resultant tiredness.
- Symptoms can recur daily, weekly, or monthly.

Main Remedies

- *Arsenicum album*
- *China officinalis*
- *Malaria officinalis*
- *Natrum muriaticum*
- *Phosphorus*

Professional treatment is required

China occidentalis – Cinchona bark

Afterword

Kate and I are proposing a dramatic departure from the accepted paradigm of "a war on disease" that currently prevails within conventional western medicine. Yet the model we've presented here speaks of instinctual wisdom that many of us already know to our very bones. The time has come to act upon this knowledge and begin to elicit authentic healing on every level.

My deepest hope is that this book will open your mind to an empowering new way to look at your child's immune system. My vision includes being able to share this message in a myriad of possible ways: with the mother next door in my local community, with the mother who speaks a different language on the other side of the globe, as well as with the mother who cannot read or write, but knows how best to love her child.

Surely the goal of having homeopathic healthcare available globally is the most effective method to provide accessible healing to all our human family regardless of race, creed, or economic condition. As a result, more vibrant health can flourish - health that does not come with a price tag serving the interests of big business or political agendas.

And even more importantly, by increasing our understanding of how viruses and bacteria contribute to the evolution of both humankind and each of us individually, we can shift our intention away from a misguided attempt to eradicate these other forms of life perceived as threatening and instead gain wisdom about how we all fit together, inextricably within the grand design. For this to occur we need worldwide endorsement of homeoprophylaxis by both local governments as well as the World Health Organization as a viable means of safe and effective disease protection.

As a healer and a mother, I share a deep connection to every mother on our planet. The love we feel for our children surpasses all understanding and springs from a deep place that cannot be defined nor measured. From this indescribable place, a powerful, intuitive wisdom compels us toward knowing how best to nurture and protect our loved ones. The information shared herein gives us not only vital knowledge, but also practical tools to employ as inspired mothers, fathers, and caretakers of tomorrow's future.

Cilla Whatcott

What Cilla and I have proposed here is not new. It is a call for us to look to the future to see if the infectious disease prevention principles and methodology in use today will serve us for generations to come. It is a call for us to look back into the history of immunological studies and pull forth the important findings of homeopaths in the mid-seventeen and eighteen hundreds. These homeopaths worked alongside the men who were championed as the discoverers of the "Germ Theory," which states that disease agents are the cause of disease. One hundred and fifty years later modern medicine still works from this premise, even though towards the end of his life, Louis Pasteur, recanted his declaration, stating it is the economy of the individual that gives way to the disease process rather than the germ.

Why was Louis Pasteur's voice of reason not heard? And today, when we are faced with the incidence of one in thirty-six U.S. children having some sort of developmental disorder, why are scientists, doctors, and public officials inefficient in their questioning the science of the vaccination, when so many parents, in front of their own eyes, have seen the deleterious and injurious effects of vaccinations to their children?

What we have here, in this book, is a glimmer of hope: hope for us to find reason once again in our attempts to keep our children healthy and strong. Infectious disease is not what is to be feared; rather it is our own ignorance in figuring out how to work with it and those that would push fear agendas upon us.

Homeoprophylaxis opens the door to a whole new level of possibility when it comes to preventing disease. Not only do the results of preliminary studies demonstrate effectiveness, but they also indicate that a higher level of health is achieved in those children who have undergone HPx. Some of the larger studies demonstrate that with a single dose of a particular nosode, disease incidence is practically eliminated in that population.

For me, this is where I begin to see the power of HPx. It is as if by some concurrence, a whole population of people is affected. Is it that the germ has been wiped out (the desire of every western doctor)? Or is it that with HPx, the need for the presence of the pathogen in that human population has been eliminated? I will let you ponder the ramifications of these thoughts as we continue our work nationally and internationally promoting the use of HPx for infectious disease prevention.

Homeoprophylaxis for free and healthy children.

Kate Birch

About the Authors

Kate Birch is a board-certified classical homeopath, registered with the North American Society of Homeopaths. She has been in private practice, currently in Minneapolis, Minnesota, since 1994. She lectures locally and internationally on the use of homeopathy for infectious disease prevention and treatment. Her practice specializes in pediatrics. She works with families who have not vaccinated in keeping their children healthy and supporting the immune system through its natural development and with children who have suffered from vaccine injury, or other developmental concerns. She has two grown children, and she loves to travel and meet people from all over the world.

Cilla Whatcott is a board-certified classical homeopath who also holds a bachelor's degree in fine arts from Arizona State University. She has a private homeopathic practice in Chaska, Minnesota and teaches classes including 'Homeopathy for Medical Professionals,' 'Homeopathy,' and 'Vaccine Awareness' at Normandale Community College in Bloomington, Minnesota. Three of her children are adopted from China, Taiwan, and Russia and she and her husband, Neal, also have one biological son born while living in the beautiful Marshall Islands. This is her first book, and her interests include cooking, sailing in tropical waters, and health and healing.

Hannah Albert is a board-certified Naturopath, homeopath, artist, author, and creative retreat leader. After 10 years of primary care practice as a Naturopathic Doctor in Seattle, Washington she has moved to Minneapolis to create more balance in her life as an artist and healer. She is inspired by the sounds of laughter, breaking waves, and owls hooting, as well as homemade food shared between friends and most things that sparkle.

Appendices

Access to Homeoprophylaxis: Freeandhealthychildren.org

Resources

Birch, Kate. – Vaccine Free Prevention & Treatment of Infectious Contagious Disease with Homeopathy

Birch, K., Sandon, S., Damlo, S., Lane, Kim – Long-term Homoeoprophylaxis Study in Children in North America: Part One and Two

Golden, Isaac. – Homeoprophylaxis - A Fifteen Year Clinical Study: A Statistical Review of the Efficacy and Safety of Long-Term Homeoprophylaxis

Golden, Isaac. – The Complete Practitioners Manual of Homeoprophylaxis

Whatcott, Cilla. – There is a Choice: Homeoprophylaxis

Neustaedter, Randall. – The Vaccine Guide: Risks and Benefits for Children and Adults
  – The Holistic Baby Guide: Alternative Care for Common Health Problems
  – The Immunization Decision: A Guide for Parents (The Family health series)
  – Flu: Alternative Treatments and Prevention

Organizations

1. Centers for Disease Control: www.cdc.gov
2. Vaccine Adverse Events Reporting System: www.vaers.hhs.gov. info@vaers.org
   PO Box 1100, Rockville, MD 20849-1100. 1-800-822-7967
3. National Vaccine Information Center: www.nvic.org.

Index

134

Sexually transmitted disease, 2, 37, 40, 44, 54, 119, 121, 122

Single dose, 39, 42, 53, 130

Smallpox, 8, 9, 35, 66

Specific immunity, 22, 73, 74

Spike protein, 16, 111

Staphylococcinum, 37

Staphylococcus, 11

Stramonium, 105, 107

Streptococcinum, 37, 42, 54

Streptococcus, 11, 13, 42, 113

Streptomyces, 13

Succussion, 35, 36

Sugar cravings, 13

Sugar pellets, 34, 53, 57, 73, 104

Supplemental nosodes, 55

Supportive remedy, 36, 39, 43, 44, 45, 52

Suppression, 18, 23, 24, 33, 34, 38, 61, 70

Susceptibility, 6, 7, 10, 12, 16, 17, 18, 23, 38, 40, 42, 43, 44, 47, 52, 53, 54, 57, 74, 76, 91, 97, 123

Syphilinum, 37

T

Tetanotoxin, 37, 42

Tetanus, 42, 52, 66, 70, 114

Th1, 22, 24, 25, 41, 42, 57, 70, 74

Th2, 22, 24, 25, 41, 42, 57, 68, 70, 74

Thimerosal, 59, 68, 73

Thuja, 121

Titer, 52, 56, 58, 60, 81

Travel HPx Program, 44, 55

Travel overseas, 2, 37, 44, 46, 55, 123, 131

Trifolium repens, 112

Triple dose, 39, 42

Tropical diseases, 2, 35, 44, 55, 103, 123

Tuberculinum, 34, 37, 42, 54

Tuberculosis, 42, 70

Typhoid, 123, 125

Typhoidinum, 37, 55

U

Unvaccinated, 76, 81, 85

V

Vaccination, ii, iii, 1, 2, 7, 25, 34, 35, 47, 51, 59, 60, 61, 64, 66, 67, 76, 77, 81, 82, 88, 97, 130

Vaccine, 1, 4, ii, 16, 18, 28, 33, 34, 36, 41, 42, 62, 66, 67, 68, 69, 76, 77, 96, 131, 132, 139

Vaccine Adverse Events Reporting System, 62, 96, 132

Vaccine schedule, 34, 54, 56, 59, 66, 70, 97, 103

Vaccinosis, 9, 35, 72

Varicella, 66

Varicella nosode, 37, 54

Varicella-zoster virus, 105

Variolinum, 35, 37

Veratrum album, 117, 124

Virus, 2, 5, 7, 9, 15, 16

Vital force, 5, 11

W

War, 5

Weight, 53

Whooping cough, 42, 59, 70, 71, 83, 113, 115

Wine, 5

World Economic Forum, 98

World Health Organization, 65, 95, 99, 129

Y

Yeast, 13, 14, 61, 67, 68

Yellow fever, 55, 123, 126, 127

Endnotes

1. Hambidge, Michael and Krebs, Nancy. "Zinc, Diarrhea and Pneumonia." Journal of Pediatrics 135 (Dec.1999):661- 664.

2. World Health Organization. "Antimicrobial Resistance and Its Global Spread." World Health Day Conference (April 2011).

3. Montagnier, Luc, et al. "Electromagnetic Signals are Produced by Aqueous Nanostructures Derived from Bacterial DNA Sequences." Interdisciplinary Sciences: Computational Life Sciences. 1 (2009): 81-90.

4. Cowan, T, Fallon, S. The Contagion Myth: Why Viruses (including "Coronavirus") Are Not the Cause of Disease. Skyhorse publishing, September 2020.

5. Birch K, Heng J, Morse C, Garrison S, Wood C, Calvi-Rooney G, Dobelmann U. The shattered mirror: synthesis of induced and cured symptoms of coronavirus nosode, Novus-CV PRC, in homoeopathic dilution in humans. The American Homoeopath, Journal of the North America Society of Homoeopaths, 2021;27.

6. Birch, Kate. "Vaccine Free Prevention and Treatment of Infectious Contagious Disease with Homeopathy." 2nd Edition. Germany: Narayana, 2010.

7. Journal of Clinical Infectious Disease. Clinical Infectious Diseases 2012:54(12):1778-83. <http:cid.ofordjournals.org/54/12/18.full.pdf>.

8. Goddard, Sally. "Reflexes, Learning and Behavior." Eugene: Fern Ridge Press, 2005.

8. Hahnemann, Samuel. "The Cure and Prevention of Scarlet Fever." Lessor Writings. B Jain Publishers, New Delhi.

9. Montagnier, Luc, et al. "Electromagnetic Signals are Produced by Aqueous Nanostructures Derived from Bacterial DNA Sequences." Interdisciplinary Sciences: Computational Life Sciences. 1 (2009): 81-90.

11. Golden, Dr. Isaac. "Homeoprophylaxis - A Fifteen Year Clinical Study: A Statistical Review of the Efficacy and Safety of Long-Term Homeoprophylaxis." Isaac Golden Publications. Gisborne. Vic. 2004.

12. Ibid.

13. Birch, K, Sandon, S, Damlo, S, Lane, K. Long-term homoeoprophylaxis study in children in North America. Part Two: Safety of HP, review of immunological responses, and effects on general health outcomes. Similia. Journal of the Australian Society of Homeopaths. June 2020.

14. Birch, Kate. Glyphosate Free. KPD Publishers, USA, 2019.

15. Brundtland, Dr. Gro Harlem. "Removing Obstacles to Healthy Development." World Health Organization, 2009. <http://www.who.int/infectious-disease-report/pages/textonly.html>.

15. Ibid.

17. Department of Health and Human Services Centers for Disease Control. "Child and Adolescent Immunization Schedule."<http://www.cdc.gov/vaccines/recs/schedules/child-schedule.html>.

18. Hooper, Edward. "The River: A Journey to the Source of HIV and AIDS." Boston: Back Bay Books, 2000.

19. Gaithersburg, MD. "Vaccines and Related Biological Products Advisory Committee." FDA Center for Biologics Evaluation and Research. 2010-05-07.

20. Scheibner, Viera, PhD. "Adverse Effects of Adjuvants in vaccines." Nexus 12-2000 & 2-2001.

21. Ibid

22. Generation Rescue, Inc. "Autism and Vaccines Around the World: Vaccine Schedules, Autism Rates, and Under 5 Mortality." Rescuepost.com. April 2009.

Generation Rescue.
<http://www.rescuepost.com/files/gr-autism_and_vaccines_world_special_report1.pdf.

23. Prevalence and Characteristics of Autism Spectrum Disorder Among Children Aged 8 Years — Autism and Developmental Disabilities Monitoring Network, 11 Sites, United States, 2020 | MMWR (cdc.gov).

24. Harris, Gardiner. "Deal in an Autism Case Fuels Debate." New York Times. March 2008.

23. McDonald, Kara, Huq, Shamina, Lix, Lisa, Becker, et al. "Delay in diphtheria, pertussis, tetanus vaccination is associated with a reduced risk of childhood asthma." Journal of Allergy and Clinical Immunology. 121 (Mar. 2008): 626-631.

26. Cell Press. "No Antibodies Required for Immunity Against Some Viruses." Medical News Today. Medi Lexicon, Intl., 3 Mar. 2012. Web. 1 Apr. 2012. <http://www.medicalnewstoday.com/relseases/24240 3.php>.

27 Montagnier, Luc, et al. "Electromagnetic Signals are Produced by Aqueous Nanostructures Derived from Bacterial DNA Sequences." Interdisciplinary Sciences: Computational Life Sciences. 1 (2009): 81-90.

26. Rubin, Steven. "Dead Babies and Stillbirths Reported to FDA after Vaccination - Mothering Magazine." therefusers.com. 2 Nov. 2011. The Refusers. <http://therefusers.com/refusers-newsroom/dead-babies-and-stillbirths- reported-to-the-fda-after-vaccination-mothering-magazine/>.

27. Reinberg, Steven. "Vaccine Not Fail-Safe in Ongoing Mumps Outbreaks." Bloomberg Businessweek. February 2010.

28. Sheldrake, Rupert. "A New Science of Life." Los Angeles: J.P. Tarcher, 1981.

31. Golden, Dr. Isaac. "Large Homoeoprophylaxis Interventions by Government Institutions." Similia, The Australian Journal of Homoeopathic Medicine. Volume 31, Number 2. Hobart, Tasmania. December 2019.

30. Golden, Dr. Isaac. "Homeoprophylaxis - A Fifteen Year Clinical Study: A Statistical Review of the Efficacy and Safety of Long-Term Homeoprophylaxis." Isaac Golden Publications. Gisborne. Vic. 2004.

33. Birch, K, Sandon, S, Damlo, S, Lane, K. Long-term homoeoprophylaxis study in children in North America. Part One: Factors contributing to the successful completion of sequential dosing of disease nosodes. Similia. Journal of the Australian Society of Homeopaths. Dec. 2019.

34. Birch, K, Sandon, S, Damlo, S, Lane, K. Long-term homoeoprophylaxis study in children in North America. Part Two: Safety of HP, review of immunological responses, and effects on general health outcomes. Similia. Journal of the Australian Society of Homeopaths. June 2020.

35. Castro, D., Nogueira, G., "Use of the nosode Meningococcinum as a preventative against meningitis." Journal of the American Institute of Homeopathy. 4 (Dec. 1968): 211-219.

36. Ibid.

37. Bandyopadhyay, Das, Sengupta, Saha, Das, Sarkar, and Nayak. "Decreased Intensity of Japanese Encephalitis Virus Infection in Chick Chorioallantoic Membrane Under Influence of Ultra-Diluted Belladonna Extract" American Journal of Infectious Diseases. 6.2 (2010): 24-28.

38. "Contribution of Homeopathy to the Control of an Outbreak of Dengue in Macaé," Rio de Janeiro Laila Aparecida de Souza Nunes Municipal Secretary of Health, Macaé, RJ, Brazil Int. J High Dilution Res 2008; 7(25):186-192.

39. Rafeeque, M. Rapid Action Epidemic Control Cell Homeopathy in India (RAECH) for Dengue. Dept of Homeopathy Government of Kerala. 2009-2001. Rapid Action Epidemic Control Cell Homeopathy in India (RAECH) for Dengue | Free and Healthy Children International.

40. Ibid.

41. Bracho, G., Varela, E., Fernandez, R., et al. "Large-scale application of highly-diluted bacteria for Leptospirosis epidemic control." Homeopathy. 99 (2010): 156-166.

42. Saine, Andre ND. "Homeopathic Prophylaxis in Epidemic Disease: History and Practice." Lecture notes: California, December 1988.

43. Offit, P. The Cutter Incident. Yale University Press. 2005. <Shining a light on POLIO | Stand for Health Freedom>

44. Hooper, Edward. "The River: A Journey to the Source of HIV and AIDS". Boston: Back Bay Books, 2000.

45. AVERT, Wes Sussex, UK. Worldwide HIV and AIDS Statistics. 2009 and 2010. <http://www.avert.org/worldstats.htm>

46. Ibid.

47. Birch, Kate. Glyphosate Free. KPD Publishers, USA, 2019.

48 Nayak D. · Devarajan K. · Pal P.P. · Ponnam H.B. · Jain N. · Shastri V. · Bawaskar R. · Chinta R. · Khurana A. Efficacy of Arsenicum album 30C in the Prevention of Covid-19 in Individuals Residing in Containment areas– A Prospective, Multicentre, Cluster-Randomized, Parallel arm, Community based, Open-label Study. October 04, 2022. https://www.karger.com/.

49. Birch, K., Heng, J., Morse, C. Garrison, S., Wood, C., Calvi-Rooney, G., Dobelmann, D. A Homeopathic Proving of the Coronavirus nosode; Novus-CV. AKA: Abbreviation Novus-CV PRC (People's Republic of China). Similia, The Australian Journal of Homoeopathic Medicine. Volume 31, Number 2. Hobert, Tasmania. Dec 2021.

50. Birch, K., Heng, J., Morse, C. Garrison, S., Wood, C., Calvi-Rooney, G., Dobelmann, D. "Determining the safety, effects, and efficacy of Novus-CV PRC in homeopathic dilution in humans for Covid-19 disease prevention." Similia, The Australian Journal of Homoeopathic Medicine. Volume 31, Number 2. Hobert, Tasmania. June 2021.

51. Birch K, Heng J, Morse C, Garrison S, Wood C, Calvi-Rooney G, Dobelmann U. The shattered mirror: synthesis of induced and cured symptoms of coronavirus nosode, Novus-CV PRC, in homoeopathic dilution in humans. The American Homoeopath, Journal of the North America Society of Homoeopaths, 2021;27.

52. Centers for Disease Control and Prevention. https://www.cdc.gov/coronavirus/2019-ncov/hcp/clinical-tips-for-healthcare-providers.html (last viewed 1.4.20).

53. Bracho, G., Varela, E., Fernandez, R., et al. "Large-scale application of highly-diluted bacteria for Leptospirosis epidemic control." Homeopathy. 99 (2010): 156-166. https://pubmed.ncbi.nlm.nih.gov/20674839/.

54 .Pappas, Pam. "Homeopathy, allopathy, and the 1918 Influenza Pandemic." Hpathy. November 8, 2010. https://hpathy.com/homeopathy-papers/homeopathy-allopathy-and-the-1918-influenza-pandemic/.

55. Golden, Isaac, PhD. "Large Homoeoprophylaxis Interventions by Government Institutions." Similia, The Australian Journal of Homoeopathic Medicine. Volume 31, Number 2. Hobert, Tasmania. December 2019. https://freeandhealthychildren.files.wordpress.com/2020/12/similia.-approved-government-programs-for-homeoprophylaxis.pdf.

56. Hahnemann, S (1997). "The Organon of Medicine." 5th Edition translated by Dudgeon. 6th Edition translated by Boericke. Paragraphs 34-40. http://www.homeoint.org/books/hahorgan/organ020.htm#P34E5. (Last viewed 1.4, 2021).

57. Center for Vaccine Ethics and Policy, University of Pennsylvania. "Global Vaccines Revenues Projected to More than Double by 2016." January 2010. <http://centerforvaccineethicsandpolicy.wordpress.com/2010/01/17/global-vaccines-revenues-projected-to-more-than-double-by-2016/>.

58. Global Vaccine Market Report <https://cdn.who.int/media/docs/default-

source/immunization/mi4a/2020_global-vaccine-market-report.pdf?sfvrsn=48a58ada_1&download=true>.

59. Nightingale SL, Prasher JM, Simonson S. Emergency Use Authorization (EUA) to enable use of needed products in civilian and military emergencies, United States. Emerg Infect Dis [serial on the Internet]. 2007 Jul [date cited]. Available from <http://wwwnc.cdc.gov/eid/article/13/7/06-1188.htm>.

60. Athey et all. The economic case for federal investment in CODIV-19 Vaccines and therapeutics remains strong. Brookings. April 2022. USC Schaeffer. <brookings.edu>.

61. Crista, Rafael Perez. Panorama of Sanitary regulations and Nosodes. Director General of regulatory agency for health protection, MINSAP, Cuba, NOSODES2008, Havana Cuba.

62. Birch, Kate. "Homeoprophylaxis for Infectious Disease." The American Homeopath 15 (2009): 69-75.

63. Golden, Dr. Isaac. "Homeoprophylaxis - A Fifteen Year Clinical Study: A Statistical Review of the Efficacy and Safety of Long-Term Homeoprophylaxis." Isaac Golden Publications. Gisborne. Vic. 2004.

64. Birch, K, Sandon, S, Damlo, S, Lane, K. Long-term homoeoprophylaxis study in children in North America. Part One: Factors contributing to the successful completion of sequential dosing of disease nosodes. Similia. Journal of the Australian Society of Homeopaths. Dec. 2019.

65. Birch, K, Sandon, S, Damlo, S, Lane, K. Long-term homoeoprophylaxis study in children in North America. Part Two: Safety of HP, review of immunological responses, and effects on general health outcomes. Similia. Journal of the Australian Society of Homeopaths. June 2020.

66. Birch, K., Heng, J., Morse, C. Garrison, S., Wood, C., Calvi-Rooney, G., Dobelmann, D. "Determining the safety, effects, and efficacy of Novus-CV in homeopathic dilution in humans for Covid-19 disease prevention." Similia, The Australian Journal of Homoeopathic Medicine. Volume 31, Number 2. Hobert, Tasmania. June 2021.

67. World Health Freedom Assembly, International Declaration of Health Freedom. St Paul, MN 2006. http://www.nationalhealthfreedom.org/documents/worldhealthfreedom_assembly.pdf.

68. Hahnemann, Samuel. "Organon of the Medical Art." Ed. Wenda Brewster O'Reilly. Palo Alto: Birdcage, 1996

Made in the USA
Monee, IL
17 May 2025

17644532R00098

THE BIG GRADUATION SHOW

The gymnasium was packed with parents. Sami stood on stage, heart pounding, as the music started. He took a deep breath and began to sing with his classmates. His voice wobbled at first, but when he saw the smiling faces in the crowd, he gained confidence and sang louder.

After the song, it was time for the certificates. Ms. Green called each student's name. 'Sami!' He walked up proudly and shook her hand. The audience cheered! 'Wow,' he whispered, staring at his shiny certificate. 'I really did it!'

When the ceremony ended, Sami felt a rush of excitement. He had done it! He had finished preschool and was ready for the next big step. But first, he had to celebrate-because a big moment like this deserved something extra special.

THE CELEBRATION BEGINS

After school, Sami skipped down the sidewalk, still holding his shiny graduation certificate. He had a big plan—celebrate with ice cream! He ran to the ice cream shop, eyes wide as he stared at all the colorful flavors. 'One giant chocolate sundae, please!' he said excitedly.

Sami found a seat near the window and dug into his sundae, the cold, chocolatey goodness making him smile. As he ate, he thought about all his preschool memories—finger painting, building the tallest block towers, and running races at recess. 'This was the best year ever!' he said between bites.

As he finished his ice cream, Sami held his graduation certificate proudly. 'I'm going to hang this on my wall!' he decided. The sun was setting as he walked home, feeling proud. The next adventure was just around the corner-but tonight was all about celebrating.

Made in the USA
Monee, IL
17 May 2025

17644391R00017